3D SUCCESS

Changing Careers in Mid Life

LINDA WEGNER

3D SUCCESS: CHANGING CAREERS IN MID LIFE

ISBN:978-1-77069-666-2

Printed in Canada

Word Alive Press
131 Cordite Road, Winnipeg, MB R3W 1S1
www.wordalivepress.ca

Library and Archives Canada Cataloguing in Publication

Wegner, Linda, 1943-

3D success : changing careers in mid-life / by Linda Wegner.

ISBN 978-1-77069-666-2

1. Career changes. 2. Middle-aged persons--Employment. I. Title.

HF5384.W44 2012 650.14 C2012-904103-3

Dedication

To Donna Crothers

As my senior editor and mentor, you held me to the highest standards of excellence; as my friend, you cheered me on in victories and supported me through times of deepest disappointment. Even as a writer I cannot fully express my appreciation.

Table of Contents

SECTION THREE: DEFENDING YOUR PRIORITIES

ACKNOWLEDGEMENTS

CITING THOSE WHO HAVE ENCOURAGED AND SUPPORTED ME IS easy; being sure I don't forget someone is another story. But with the realization that I could never name all those who have helped me on this journey, I begin:

Ron Johnson, Darryl Craig and Ken Stephenson: you helped guide those first faltering steps, and for that I will always be grateful.

To Don Allan: thank you for being a friend, business colleague and mentor. You made it possible to expand my professional services while gaining new confidence in my own skills.

Diana Lamont, professional accountant and treasured friend: thank you for maintaining my financial records with such excellence.

My colleagues at OTR Global: it was a tremendous opportunity to work with such a great team; you contributed to my success in ways you will never know.

To Mark MacDonald: thank you for giving me the opportunity to write for *Invest Northwest Publishing Company*, and to Shawn, Joanne, Robert and Ezra. It's been a privilege to be co-workers with you.

To Cathy and Peter at *Country Life in BC:* thanks for the privilege of writing for you. Thanks, too, for inviting me to contribute my monthly column, Wanna Be Farmer. Being part of the team is an honour and a lot of fun.

To the editors and owners of *Estevan Lifestyles, Carlyle Observer, Weyburn This Week* and *Battlefords Publishing Ltd*: thank you for running my weekly article all these years; I look forward to my Sunday evening opportunities to express my heart.

To Isabelle, my friend, neighbour and owner and publisher of *Powell River Living:* Thank you for asking me to contribute to the publication, and even more thanks for inviting me to be part of your life. Nor can I forget to thank you, Sean, for your constant encouragement and help.

To Pam Krompocker and staff at Powell River Community Futures: thank you for your support, especially over those first challenging years. You made reaching my goals a little easier to achieve.

To Lyn Adamson and staff at Powell River Career Link: it was your willingness to incorporate my workshop into your programs that spawned the idea and inspiration for this book.

To the many friends I've met through time spent in various Board of Director positions: you have demonstrated skills and personal commitments that make me realize what it takes to turn an organization into a success.

To our local Toastmasters clubs: the benefits I've gained through membership in both clubs have been beyond my expectations.

Last, but far from least, thanks to my family and friends who have stood with me and supported me over the past twelve years: I couldn't have done it without you.

Foreword

As a career development practitioner, working primarily with older workers, I have read many career resources and self-help guides. This book is different.

3D Success: Changing Careers in Midlife takes the process of career change out of the realm of theory and places it where it belongs—in the midst of busy, challenging, and sometimes messy lives. The book is full of practical, down-to-earth tips taken from the author's own experience. When I met Linda, this stay-at-home mom and pastor's wife was in the process of reinventing herself as an entrepreneur. Many of the lessons she learned on this journey of self-discovery were hard-won. One of her most impactful statements is that "Changing careers is not for cowards." These are words of wisdom from someone gifted with a rare ability to examine herself and the situation honestly. Not only did Linda face her own struggles courageously, she somehow gives us—the readers—the courage to face them too.

Another thing that makes this book different is the way Linda cautions us to consider the needs of other people in our lives: partners, family members, colleagues. Too many self-help guides assume that people operate in a vacuum, freely making decisions while taking only themselves into account.

In my experience, this is a risky endeavour. Family members can, either innocently or deliberately, scuttle plans that were made without considering their needs. One of the book's real strengths is Linda's insistence on placing the reader within the larger context of community.

Count the cost. Many people in the midst of career change skip this step, to their detriment. Blithely stepping off into the unknown, without considering what may have to be jettisoned, is unwise. There are many pitfalls on the path of career change. It may cut into family time or have a lasting and negative impact on finances. There may not be a market for the services offered. Entrepreneurs may face a long start-up period, in which they are forced to rely on the paycheque of another family member. To her great credit, Linda is aware of the pitfalls, and makes sure the reader is aware of them too. She speaks with admirable honesty about her own struggles: the tears, the self-doubt, and even the doubts expressed by friends. Luckily, these were balanced by unfailing support from her mentors and by her own significant inner strength.

From a structural point of view, among the things I appreciated most were the sections entitled "Lessons I've Learned" and "Something to Think About" that appear at the end of every chapter. These can be consulted again and again by the reader as a quick reference guide to the process of career change.

As a believer, I also appreciated the spiritual dimension. The path of career change is a challenging and sometimes lonely one. It's helpful to have a Friend along the way.

While this book was written for all those on the path of career change, I believe it will be particularly helpful for those considering self-employment. Linda has built a successful business from the ground up. I have watched as, over and over again, she mentored others with the same hopes and ambitions. She is a credit to our community.

In conclusion, I would like to thank Linda Wegner for undertaking this project. She is a true success story—a person who, with her head full of dreams, still manages to keep her feet firmly on the ground.

–Susan Young de Biagi, Author and Certified Career Development Practitioner

PREFACE

I HAD TWO PURPOSES IN MIND WHEN I SET OUT TO WRITE THIS book: the first, simply to record my story, and the other to communicate the lessons I've learned to others. If you, like me, are facing the challenge of beginning a new phase of your life, I'd love the privilege of sharing a few things I've learned about navigating a midlife career change and, in particular, about launching your own business. It's my journey, but I know I am in the company of many fellow travellers.

From the first word that appeared on my computer screen to this, a published book, I have proclaimed myself a learner, anything but a formally trained "expert." I launched my company boasting a grade twelve education (although I did graduate with honours), a Certificate of Ordination, and a fiery determination not to let my circumstances get the best of me. I was fifty-seven years of age, scared and fragile, the day I hung out my symbolic shingle. As I write this, I'm twelve years older, my shingle has been primed and painted, I rarely feel scared anymore and I feel stronger than ever.

I would be remiss if I included only the business-related portion of my story, however. While religious faith doesn't necessarily have anything to do with creating a budget, marketing products, or joining the Chamber of Commerce, there were many days when only the presence of Jesus Christ in my life provided me with the inner strength and courage to keep going when it would have been so easy to quit.

If you are of another—or no—religious faith or affiliation, the information in this book remains pertinent to the topic. The text centres on the how-to and the few references to faith are mostly contained in the Lessons I Have Learned During This Process section of each chapter. It is here, in this Preface, that I voice my heart's desire to give glory to my faithful Saviour, Lord and Friend.

Here's my story: After nearly thirty years of vocational ministry, a vocation I loved in spite of its many challenges and frustrations, my husband's health broke. There is no need to go into the details but suffice it to say in the matter of a few weeks our lives were turned upside-down: no job, no home (the mixed blessing of living in parsonages), and for me, continued health issues associated with my then-recent battle with cancer. In the days when I was trained, clergy were not supposed to yield to negativity and if they did, they certainly weren't to let anyone else know about it. Never had I felt so alone.

We packed up, left our small community and settled in a rented apartment in a city totally new to us. I still remember the day I watched the only life I knew and some of my dearest friends disappear in the rearview mirror. Exiting a community of 700 people to take up residence in the largest city in the province was, in itself, daunting.

I allowed myself less than a week to indulge in self-pity and then got busy trying to find work. Calling on my hobby of writing for several rural newspapers and lots of experience as a public speaker, I launched my company, Words of Worth (WOW). I contacted publications for whom I'd done occasional writing, garnering a number of assignments. I submitted a proposal to the Agricultural Institute of Management in Saskatchewan and to my delight was immediately offered a one-year contract as a workshop consultant. For the next number of years I had the great privilege of traveling across that wonderful province speaking to rural farm groups on the topic of stress management. To say it was a "learn as you go" project is an understatement of major proportions.

To say I worked hard is definitely another understatement. Three years later, with the support of friends and family, we purchased a home in the same community where our children lived. It was good to be near family, but now I struggled with re-establishing my business away from my contacts in the rolling prairies I loved and re-focusing on developing new clients in a geographically isolated and ferry-dependent city on the shores of the Pacific Ocean. No more mega-agriculture to write about now!

It's been nearly thirteen years since those first tentative (desperate is probably closer to the truth) calls to editors and administrators; looking back I can hardly believe the changes that have taken place in my life. I have gained confidence in my acquired skills and in my formerly non-existent ability to manage administrative duties, handle our personal financial planning needs (let alone those of my fledgling company), business communication, and the hiring and training of a team of subcontractors. I will never cease to be thankful for my mentors, Ron, Ken, Don, and Donna, and for OTR Global, the San Francisco-based company I worked with for nearly a decade. I can't even begin to name all those who supported and believed in me.

As painful as this journey has been, being forced to abandon my role in vocational ministry has been a source of spiritual growth I could not have imagined possible. I was driven to depend on Christ, and for that I can say, "Every step of the journey has been worth it because there is nothing more valuable than learning to know Him better."

As I look back with gratitude on the good things that happened over those years, I know without a doubt that it was not my hard work alone that accomplished anything. Over and over again I cried out to the Lord for strength, for encouragement and for clients; over and over again He poured out all I asked for and more. There are so many I can thank for the success of my company, but none more than the One I love above all others, the Lord Jesus Christ.

Introduction

"Middle age is when your age starts to show around your middle."

—Bob Hope

Opinions differ on the definition of middle age, but for the purposes of this book middle age is defined as being between the ages of forty-five and sixty-four. If you fit into that age bracket and you've got a well-padded resume, it only seems logical that a new employer will see you as the answer to his or her employee prayers. After all, you've got life experience, work experience, and acquired skills. You've also got the resume or CV to prove it. In addition to all that, your personal reasons for changing careers make you highly motivated. Those reasons might fit into one or more of the following categories:

- You're the result of corporate or company downsizing
- You've gone as far as you can or want to in your current work
- You're dealing with health issues or physical limitations
- You've decided it's time to follow a personal employment dream

- You want to create a work schedule that allows for a life for yourself
- You're close to retirement and your finances need some help

It's important to realize that though the challenges connected with changing careers in midlife are real, there's good news.

> Trying to find a job in mid-life can be a disheartening task. But older workers take heed: your age and experience may work for you in the market rather than against you. Employers no longer hire people with an expectation that they will be able to work for years and years. Even younger workers don't tend to stay in one position or one job for more than a few years at a time. This is good news for older workers, whose life and work experience are often welcomed in any work environment, sometimes in preference to younger workers.[1]

In spite of that encouraging note, the sad reality is that the global economy is still soft and unemployment rates seem stuck at uncomfortably high levels across North America. Not only that, often younger, more technologically savvy workers who are willing to work at entry-level jobs sometimes have advantages in the job market. Put together, that means changing careers in midlife can be particularly challenging. Gone are the days when lifetime employment, complete with a secure pension and benefits, was the norm. Perhaps you survived the latest round of cuts but you're not sure about what's coming up and you

---

[1] Calgarypubliclibrary.com (2012) Is Older Actually Better?—Work in Mid-Life and Beyond. [online] Available at: http://calgarypubliclibrary.com/blogs/career-employment-resources?p=2457#p2457.

want to be prepared by moving on before more layoffs become a reality.

Maybe you're at that stage of your life when you know you want or you've got to keep on working (and that can be a healthy thing) but you're not convinced that your current occupation is where you'd like to continue. You're looking for something new, something that will fulfill both the demands you face and the longings you're experiencing. The dream of pursuing that special occupation is still very much alive.

Let's face it: many of us wrestle both with the financial present as well as our economic futures. Even in our country, with its many social benefits, the search for different or additional employment opportunities sometimes has an aura of desperation about it. The cost of everyday living, helping our children get an education, making mortgage payments, operating a vehicle, and—if there's anything left over—planning for that far-off retirement isn't for the faint-hearted. When "I have to make changes" can be translated as "too much month at the end of the money," finding a way to supplement current revenue streams falls somewhere between attractive and essential.

This decision is even more challenging for the sandwich generation charged with the care of aging or infirm parents. Earning a living while combining those responsibilities may require the kind of flexibility not available in your current job, and that may be the tipping point that sends you seeking a change in career.

Few human beings do not, at some point in their lives, think about the job they'd really like to have, the hobby they'd like to pursue, or the legacy they'd like to leave. Unfortunately, abandoning the demands of reality in favour of a dream can have dire consequences if that decision hasn't been well thought-out, well-researched, well-planned, and a host of other "well" imperatives. There are legitimate and non-legitimate reasons for risking a lot in order to gain even more.

On the other hand, reasons for changing careers may be positive and affirming. Perhaps you have transferrable skills and you've already built a solid base of expertise. You've earned the respect of your co-workers or peers but now it's time to move on. Or rather than investing time, energy, and finances into an unrelated career path, you're interested in utilizing and expanding your existing strengths in a different setting.

For some, the opportunity of working fewer hours in a less structured work schedule or the elimination of travel to and from work may be attractive options for launching a home-based professional consultancy or business. For others, the thought of working in pyjamas until noon is reason enough.

In any case, changing careers isn't for cowards.

The reason for changing careers was, for me, simply financial. For thirty years I'd been a stay-at-home mom, pastor's wife, community volunteer, hobby writer, and specialist at doing odd jobs for minimum compensation. That all changed suddenly for me. Facing reality, I realized I had no other option but to generate enough monthly revenue to keep food on the table and gas in the car. As if that wasn't enough, I faced ongoing health problems as a result of cancer and the treatments involved. I was grateful to be alive but, I freely admit, nearly overcome with the challenges before me.

Perhaps your reasons are different: you may simply want a change or, like me, your reasons for seeking a new career path might be more complex. Whatever the reason, it's important to clearly identify why you've embarked on your new journey and where you want to end up. Your reasons may be totally different than mine or the examples I'll use throughout this book, but they are your needs and they need to be identified.

These next chapters outline the steps I've taken in changing careers. I don't pretend that they are the final word or even the next-to-final word on the subject, but they are an honest recounting of what worked for me and what didn't. This book is not, and was never intended to be, an academic textbook. For those contemplating a career change, this book simply chronicles my journey through the maze of validation, discovery, and persistent action; the validation of my known strengths; the discovery of those strengths I did not know existed; and the development of a determined plan of action that did not include quitting. I took aim at victory.

I'm not afraid to tell you where I've failed, where I wish I'd done things differently, or where I found myself cheering over a victory. But I do so with the sincere wish that by sharing the lessons I have learned, you will find your journey a bit easier.

1 SECTION

Discovering Your Passion

1 Where Are You Coming From?

"To be successful, the first thing to do is to fall in love with your work."

—Author Unknown

VIRGINIA[2] WORKED AT AN ENTRY-LEVEL PUBLIC SERVICE POSITION for nearly a decade. She'd become fed up with the political environment, including labour union issues, and decided she'd had enough. She also wanted to quit smoking. When an election was called, Virginia volunteered many after-work hours in a local campaign office. Not only did the party she worked for get elected, she also kicked the nicotine habit.

A few weeks later, Virginia was delighted to receive an unexpected invitation to work for the candidate she'd helped. She was given the opportunity to choose her position from a number available, a choice she made based not so much on compensation but on the role she was to dub her "dream job."

Though Virginia's situation may seem like a Cinderella story, making the decision to pursue a dream is one of any number of valid reasons to pursue a new career or begin your own business.

---

[2] Not her real name

In this quest to establish yourself in a different job or career, the first step is to identify your reasons for making the change. Next, identify your strengths and weaknesses and determine how they factor into your choice. By doing these things, you prepare yourself to rationally evaluate the risks and possibilities needed to move forward. Focus on the *why* before the *how.*

Look for clues everywhere. What stirs your imagination? What projects would you love to work on? Who are the people and/or their work that you most admire? Why do certain activities make you happy? What causes you to pay attention to the things that bring fulfillment or that you find most enjoyable?

The first step in this process is to **dare to dream and focus on the things you love to do**. Write down those things, no matter how improbable or unattainable they may seem. Imagine that you are standing at the proverbial intersection of where you're coming from and where you're going. The challenge lies in making sure you know where you need to go before you take off into the unknown. The old problem of "when in doubt, do something" often leads to greater confusion and difficulty than what you're facing right now.

When making your decisions, be on the lookout for clues that will help you:

- What concepts/projects make you want to be involved or take actions?
- Who are the people you most admire and why?
- What activities do you find most enjoyable?

Discovering the right "fit" for my new career was relatively easy: I already had solid writing success, a portfolio of publishing by-lines, and was comfortable speaking in front of audiences. I had no difficulty meeting strangers and was able to communicate with people who led lifestyles or held views that were different than mine. What I didn't have was formal education past high school. In addition, a major barrier to applying for many job positions was my ongoing health concerns. When I weighed my options, it looked like launching my own business was the best one.

After eliminating other possibilities and measuring my qualifications, I began to dream of a situation where earning the supplementary income I needed would be accomplished by doing the things I loved best: communicating encouragement and information to others through the mediums of print and the spoken word. I had a long and challenging journey ahead of me, but I was ready to begin.

The emerging dream began to gain substance and form. To change careers was not an option; the direction I was to take would eventually provide choices I could never have imagined. Although it took several months, I chose my company name, *Words of Worth*, to reflect exactly what I wanted to offer the world.

A word of caution: daring to dream is not the same as passively daydreaming or conjuring ideas that are never acted upon. The first steps in turning your dream into reality involve identifying your demonstrated interests, strengths, talents, and personality type. These baby steps are vital in determining the direction you'll need to take, but they're also just the first of many miles—oops, kilometres—ahead.

Lessons I've Learned

- Focus on the things you love to do—or, as a writer once said, the things you simply cannot "not do."
- Dreams can become reality, but they don't come easily and certainly not without a lot of counsel, a willingness to yield your plans to your Heavenly Father, setbacks, and plain old-fashioned hard work.

- Dreams come true, step by step. Success in one giant leap is rare.
- The shape of a dream can change throughout the process of reaching for a goal.
- Honour each of your acquired skills and abilities; they're probably transferrable to your new career.
- Be willing to invest time and finances into training and/or classes that will increase your knowledge and skill.

SOMETHING TO THINK ABOUT

I invite you to work through the following exercises. Happy discovery!

A first step in discovering your personal personality traits, your talents, skills, and preferences can be as simple as asking yourself the following questions.

1. If you had an evening off, what would you rather do?

a) Go to a party

b) Stay home and surf the Internet

c) Spend time enjoying your favourite hobby

d) Go to a movie

2. Which section of the newspaper do you turn to first?

a) Advice column or letters to the editor

b) News

c) Sports

d) Entertainment

3. What would you prefer to do at a party?

a) Greet people at the door

b) Join in a discussion of current events

c) Make hors d'oeuvres

d) Entertain

4. Which book would you rather receive as a gift?

a) *Chicken Soup for the Soul*

b) *A Brief History of Time*

c) *How Things Work*

d) An art book for your coffee table

5. What would you rather do in your spare time?

a) Catch up with friends over coffee

b) Organize your closets

c) Garden or do home renovations

d) Write poetry

6. It's your turn to choose the movie. What's your first choice?

a) A romantic comedy such as *Sleepless in Seattle*

b) A thought-provoking drama such as *A Beautiful Mind*

c) An action-adventure movie such as *Star Wars*

d) An independent film such as *What the Bleep Do We Know?*

7. You're at a social event. Who would you rather join?

a) A large group that is laughing a lot

b) A small group having a lively discussion

c) Several people playing a game such as pool or darts

d) An individual who looks interesting

8. You have the chance to be on a reality show. You choose:

a) A show where your interpersonal skills can help you win, such as *Survivor, The Apprentice,* or *The Bachelor.*

b) A show where you can win on the basis of your talent, such as *American Idol, Last Comic Standing,* or *Project Runway.*

c) A show that gives you the chance to work hands-on to improve something, such as *Trading Spaces or Handyman Superstar Challenge.*
d) None. You think reality shows are a mindless waste of time.

9. Which of the following would your friends say best describes you?
a) A people person
b) Intelligent
c) Handy
d) Creative

Your answers can give you some clues to your ideal career. While virtually all careers involve working with people, information and things, and many allow some creativity, most careers focus on one particular aspect and most of us have a distinct preference.

If you answered mostly **A's**, your ideal career probably involves working with **people**. This may involve career such as mentoring, negotiation, instructing, consulting, supervising, persuading, speaking, serving, or assisting.

If you answered mostly **B's**, your ideal career probably involves working with **information**. These careers may include tasks such as synthesizing, coordinating, analyzing, compiling, computing, copying, or comparing, and career choices include library assistant, editor, web developer, professional organizer, accountant, or private investigator.

If you answered mostly **C's**, your ideal career probably involves working with **things**. Tasks you might do in these careers include setting up, precision working, controlling, driving, operating, tending, feeding or handling. Possible career choices include chef, cake decorator, repair person, carpenter, antiques dealer, dog trainer, or mechanic.

If you answered mostly **D's**, your career choice is probably **creative**. Possible career choices include writer, photographer, musician, interior decorator, graphic artist, or fashion designer.

Of course, there are many more careers to choose from, but knowing your preferred type can help you narrow down the choices.

Special thanks to Tag and Catherine Goulet for permission to use the above quiz. Visit their website at www.FebJob.com.

Job Autobiography

Inventory

For every job you've had, beginning with the earliest (e.g. babysitting, delivering newspapers), and including any volunteer work and/or homemaking/parenting, write out:

- What you liked about it
- What you didn't like about it
- Why you took it
- Why you left

Once you've done that, pick out the factors that seemed important to you and were common to all the jobs. Write down the factors and the theme.

A few more questions:

- If time and/or money were no object, what would you pursue as your life's career? Why? What aspect of that career would interest you the most?
- What do you really enjoy doing and where do your talents lie?
- What type of work brings you the most personal satisfaction?

- Do you want to continue in your current life pattern for the rest of your life?

Carefully match the list of your skills and strengths with your dreams and aspirations. As part of your plan of action (the next chapter in this book), discuss your findings with a career planning consultant or trusted and knowledgeable mentor.

2 Where Are You Going?

"For many people a job is more than an income, it's an important part of who we are. So a career transition of any sort is one of the most unsettling experiences you can face in your life."

—*Paul Clitheroe*

Now that you're taken time to discover the beauty and diversity of your innate talents and personality traits, your acquired skills, and the career you'd like to pursue while you are still in your productive working years, it's time to set your course of action. Simply parking by the side of the road, convinced you need to alter your course, is not enough. You need to know where you're ultimately headed. You've decided the direction, but now it's time to focus on taking the right road. Although you don't have all the details worked out, be clear about the things you want to change in your career.

If you've ever struggled with less than perfect vision, you know how frustrating it is to try to decipher something you can't see clearly. Pin down, as close to exactly as possible, the goal you're aiming for. Once you see the target clearly, you know where to aim the shots. This part is not an optional luxury, it's essential to your success.

Goal-setting is both an institutional type of project with templates, suggestions, and guidelines readily available, and a highly personalized exercise that incorporates your dreams and desires. It would be much easier if that was all there was to it, but the reality is your new goal also demands that you take into consideration the needs of those who figure prominently in your world. Setting goals requires a lot of soul searching.

What will you gain by heading in this new direction? If you're to stick with them, the reasons must be positive, attractive, compelling, and appealing. Heaven knows there will be potholes in the road … you'll need to have a heartfelt desire and a clear-thinking mind to get you where you're going.

How will this new direction benefit you? Obviously the answer to that question is tied up with your initial decision to change careers … but there may be more benefits than you envisioned. For me, the need to provide an income was overriding, but the unforeseen friendships I made, the places I've visited, the people I've met, and the lessons I've learned provided the proverbial icing on life's cake.

I have always loved rural life and especially rural life in an agricultural setting. Indeed, the most profound and impactful things I've learned are from the soil and the dedicated farmers and gardeners who "love the dirt." One lesson in particular stands out: in preparing to write an article about the marriage of technology and agriculture (known as Precision Farming), I spoke with a local farmer friend who'd recently acquired a behemoth of a tractor. It was a technological wonder complete with air conditioning, stereo system, the latest in GPS and every other form of technology known to tractors. Standing beside the machine, neither he nor I were as tall as the massive tires that moved the beast. After commenting on the size and capabilities of the machine, my friend replied in what seemed like a lament, "Yes, but the bigger the machine, the farther away from the dirt I am."

As you set out to reach your goal, you'll experience high mountain peaks and low valleys, so be prepared to deal with both. My sacrifices included missing certain events because of work deadlines (when you own the company there is no escaping the consequences of missed deadlines). Because I live on the West Coast of Canada and many of the clients I worked with were on the East Coast of North America, interviewing them in the morning meant getting up at 5:00 a.m. and, consequently, turning down invitations for more than one evening event I longed to attend.

It's also essential that you pin down what you really want in this new career. You can't possibly predict all that will take place during the process of getting there, but without a clearly defined objective, creating a plan becomes virtually impossible. Having a clear vision of what you want also provides you with a more positive point of view. As we'll discuss later, that alone will help you stand out to lenders, recruiters, and prospective clients.

LESSONS I'VE LEARNED

- Spend time learning all you can about your new career.
- Too often I cheated myself by forfeiting time to think because I had "too much to do." When I slowed down and allowed myself time to mull things over, I became much more productive, creative, and healthy in every way.
- Some days, the only thing that kept me going was knowing why and where I was headed.
- Much of the time I wasted on some tempting side-road

appeared to be unproductive, but the lessons I learned were invaluable.

- Avoid unproductive side-roads; it's much better to learn those valuable lessons in a less painful way.
- There is no such thing as "easy" in this process, and yet there is nothing more rewarding than making progress.
- Correction: there are "gifts" along the way when, unexpectedly, a door opens and we achieve a measure of success that we hadn't counted on coming so easily.
- Mom's words were true: nothing worth having comes easy.
- Life isn't fair, so suck it up.

Something to Think About

Create an imaginary travel map. Using a discarded atlas or a Google search, choose a destination you've always wanted to visit. Tear out or print out the map and grab one coloured pen, one regular pen, and a piece of paper. You're ready to start.

First, determine the shortest route from where you are to where you're going. Find out all you can about the major route, the available points of interest along the way and the destination of secondary highways or rural roads. Write down the main roads you plan to travel, but also any side roads that may offer valuable or long-desired information. Make a list of things you'd like to learn along the way. Now estimate the most efficient and realistic route and the time you will need to make the most of the trip.

Based on those observations, create a detailed estimate of the costs involved: food, transportation, and accommodation. Factor in a twenty percent overrun for costs, and build those numbers into a budget appropriate for your time schedule.

Finally, highlight your chosen route so that you will never stray too far off your plan. Why on Earth am I having you draw up this imaginary travel plan? Because you have now produced a good template for your business plan. Your destination is a new career or business, and just like being a good tourist, you need to plan out every detail to make a successful journey.

Here's an example:

Travel from Vancouver, British Columbia, to Winnipeg, Manitoba:

The shortest distance would be to travel by TransCanada Highway #1, 2,294 kilometers (approximately 1,426 miles). We would have to factor in the costs for fuel, wear and tear on the automobile, at least one night in a motel, and foods along the way.

Should we decide to take another route, additional costs would then be considered, but there could be benefits well worth the extra money. That's where strategies have to be considered and choices made.

Although this is a hypothetical situation, it is a good comparative picture of factors that need to be considered in your business plan. Every financial choice you make should be weighed against factors including but not limited to the following:

Necessity: while some items, such as a business licence, are non-negotiable, others can be decided based upon price vs. value to your business.

Time spent in arriving at your career destination: you may need to take additional training in order to be on top of your market. This is not wasted time, but there may be associated costs that need to be factored into your budget.

3 How Are You Going to Get There?

"You cannot plow a field by turning it over in your mind."

—Unknown

Glenys[3] worked to help support herself and her aged mother. Long days and little social life too often resulted in her drinking alone in the evenings. After finally recognizing and beating her addiction, she realized she had to make some major changes in her life. By taking advantage of the opportunity to re-enter the workforce via a local employment counseling office, she found the courage to launch her own business and her new life.

I asked Glenys what motivated her to make the change. "I did it for myself," she said.

Ted* was a successful carpenter and business owner. Now in his mid-fifties, he realized his years of hard physical labour and trying to keep up with managing a successful business were catching up with him. He simply wanted to work for someone else in a less demanding job.

Both Glenys and Ted were making changes *toward* a better life for themselves, not merely *away from* a former job.

---

[3] Not their real names

There is something incredibly exciting about finding your niche and expressing the talents, abilities, and traits that define who you are. You've identified the direction you want to go, you've already hit some snags in the road and you're aware there are more difficulties are ahead. The important thing is you're on your way.

Now the hard work of plotting your course begins in earnest. Although procrastination has sounded the death knell of many a future success story, rushing into a major decision without doing your homework has its own set of pitfalls. This is where dreaming has to be translated into documenting and doing. It's the place where ideas have to give way to reliable and applicable information. You've worked through the decision-making process and you know the direction you want to follow. The next step is to create and adhere to a work plan.

- You're ready to tackle the next challenge because you have years of training, experience, and education to back you up.
- You're ready to move on because you've acquired wisdom as well as knowledge by virtue of having lived for more than four decades.
- You're ready to launch that new business because, whether or not you're a great risk-taker, you know what you want and you want to get going.
- You're grateful for the support of someone else who believes in you. There may only be one or there may be many … or there might not be anyone you can think of. In that case, believe in yourself. You know you can do this.
- You've determined your goal, initiated those first tentative plans, moved ahead, taken risks … now FUEL THE PASSION AND GO FOR IT!

MOVE TOWARD TO WHAT YOU WANT RATHER THAN AWAY FROM WHAT YOU DON'T.

Now for the next big questions: How am I going to get there? When am I going to get there? Who can help me? How can they help?

There are a number of factors to consider in planning how you will reach your goal. Among them are the following:

- Format: to move to another employment situation or to start your own business?
- Demand: is there demand for your product or service?
- Investment: if you start your own business, can you secure the amount of time and money you are able or willing to invest?
- Purpose: are your personal goals and definition of success solidly fixed in your heart and mind?

For some, a small home-based business is their goal; for others, an executive position in an existing company. Some may want to work shorter, more flexible hours, while other, Type A individuals thrive on building a demanding business or career.

It's inevitable that days will come when you wonder why you ever embarked on this career change chaos, days when you are not sure you'll ever be able to reach your goal. Even worse, you may begin to berate yourself for having launched such a risky venture. That's the time to pull out that list of benefits you compiled early on in the process.

KEEP THE VISION OF WHERE YOU WANT TO GO IN VIEW.

Whether it's through inspirational books or speeches, journal entries or creating a wall-mounted plan for success, it's vital to keep focused on your goal. There will be delays, detours, distractions, and unexpected challenges along the way, but if you know where you're headed you can negotiate the bends in the road.

In his book, *The Power to Soar Higher,* Peter Legge sums it up:

> Changing direction isn't the same thing as quitting or failure; rather, it is an acknowledgement that what you've been doing up to now isn't giving you what you want or need in life. Just because you begin your career in one field doesn't mean you can't change and do something else when you discover what your true passion is.[4]

DEVELOP PLANS OF ACTION.

You need several kinds of plans: a personal agenda, a date/timeline of things to do, and most importantly, a business plan. Chapter Seven looks at the process involved in creating a business plan.

LESSONS I'VE LEARNED

- Be patient with yourself. Finding your right career path may take time; developing the necessary framework for setting out on that new path certainly will.
- Remain focused, don't panic.
- Allot time for quiet meditation; make it an integral part of your plan to achieve what you set out to do.
- Learn to turn to your support system when you need advice or encouragement.
- Surround yourself with people who know more than you do.

---

[4] Legge, Peter, *The Power To Soar Higher,* Eaglet Publishing, 2009, p. 45

SOMETHING TO THINK ABOUT

It's time to get out your literal or virtual felt pens, scissors, and paste.

Based on the list of strengths, talents, and skills you've identified and the goal you want to reach, create a banner. Whether you choose to use paper, fabric, or technology, the banner needs to be viewed easily and should contain the following information:

- Who you are
- What's important to you
- What you want in your future career

You'll need to narrow down and distill the information so that the themes and important features are not lost in masses of detail. In other words, make sure the most important information stands out; every time you look at this banner you want to be reminded of your goals.

You'll also need to make the words large enough that they can be easily seen.

No matter the medium, use virtual graphics or pictures drawn or cut from print media, and text that communicates the themes that are significant to you. Suggestions include text or pictures/graphics that identify:

- Your personality type
- Your individual and relationship values
- Themes and particular interests that are important to you
- Your significant strengths and skills
- Your personal limitations: e.g. health concerns, hours of work per week, whether you're willing to do shift work, sedentary or active work, etc.
- Your choice of working conditions: for others or launching your own business

- Wage and benefits expectations, financial options or limitations
- Don't worry about creating a work of art; it is a tool to communicate to yourself and others what's important to you and what you want to achieve.

4 What Are You Willing to Change?

"Those who expect moments of change to be comfortable and free of conflict have not learned their history."

—Joan Wallach Scott

One of the self-imposed directives I have given myself reads like this: if you can't climb mountains, try some hills. If those are too steep, maintain a steady pace. The important thing is to make sure you keep on walking. There can be no change of career without some changes of attitude and thought. Consider these words:

> It is not the critic who counts; not the man who points out how the strong man stumbled or where the doer of deeds could have done them better. The credit belongs to the man who is actually in the arena; whose face is marred by dust and sweat and blood; who strives valiantly; who errs, and comes short again and again, because there is no effort without error and shortcoming; who does actually try to do the deed; who knows the great enthusiasm, the great devotion and

> spends himself in a worthy cause; who, at the worst, if he fails, at least fails while daring greatly.
> Far better is it to dare mighty things, to win glorious triumphs even though checkered by failure, than to rank with those poor spirits who neither enjoy nor suffer much because they live in the gray twilight that knows neither victory nor defeat.[5]

Changing careers is no different. Even when things are going well, you will experience moments of discouragement. Even if you are enjoying a measure of success, something unexpected could pop up at the least convenient time. Even when others are congratulating you or cheering you on, there will be moments of self-doubt and negative thinking.

Denyse O'Leary, Canadian journalist and author of several award-winning books, outlines what she calls "career killers":

> I just didn't have the time.
> *Translation: I didn't care enough to make the time.*
>
> I didn't think I'd succeed.
> *Translation: I was unwilling to plan for success.*
>
> I didn't think anyone would take me seriously.
> *Translation: I don't take myself seriously.*
>
> Other people said I should do something else.
> *Translation: God didn't give me a vocation. He just told me to keep busy.*

---

[5] Former President Franklin Roosevelt, *Quotations from the speeches and other works of Theodore Roosevelt*, http://www.theodoreroosevelt.org/life/quotes.htm

My mother-in-law's business partner's hairdresser said my writing was no good.
Translation: I accept freelance putdowns from just about anybody. [6]

Overcoming negative thinking begins with baby steps, as in learning to replace:

I can't… with I *won't*
I should… with I *could*
It's not my fault… with *I'm responsible*
It's a problem… with it's *an opportunity*
Life's a struggle… with life's *an adventure*
I'm never satisfied … with *I want to learn and grow*
I hope … with I *know*
If only … with *next time*
What will I do? … with *I know I can handle it*
It's terrible … with it's *a learning experience*

In addition to the habits of self-doubt and negative thinking, self-deception can interfere with forward action. One of our most difficult personal challenges is to face ourselves and get a clear picture of our motivations and judgments. Ironically, it is the things we criticize in others that we excuse in ourselves. When it comes to personality, it's far too easy to let ourselves off the hook because "that's just how we are." Here's an honest confession of my struggle with a personality trait that is both a strength and weakness.

I'm Type A personality, a race horse chomping at the bit to get out of the starting gate and into the race. The trouble is that over the years I've sometimes been more like a messenger

[6] O'Leary, *Surviving and Succeeding as a Freelance Writer*, workshop presentation material, used with permission.

tearing around the track without a message. Forcing myself to focus on a specific goal was important. Of equal importance, however, was learning not to take on more than I could handle, be it work assignments or other pursuits. I made some really bad decisions, but because of lessons learned through those mistakes, the counsel of experienced business friends, and the presence of my business plan, I was able to move past my mistakes and keep on growing in my own and in my company's life.

You may not share my challenges, but perhaps you tend to be plagued with a kind of navel-gazing and indecisive personality. Procrastination, fear of trying new things, hesitancy and/or a lack of motivation are as potentially destructive as unrestrained impulsiveness.

Whether you have started your own business, are looking for other employment or have already started your new career with an existing company, a positive attitude is an asset that suits any and all personalities. It's just as important to realize that an attitude of "just good enough" will never take anyone beyond the level of mediocrity!

While interviewing a business owner for a magazine article, I asked him what message he wanted his company to send to its current and potential customers and suppliers. "Perfect is good enough," he told me. "That's our motto." Furthermore, he meets with his staff each morning to discuss the upcoming day and to remind himself and them of the importance of stellar customer service and quality of products. Not surprisingly, he owns and operates a very successful agricultural business in the Province of British Columbia.

As a sometimes employer in contract-specific projects, I watch carefully for signs of an "it's good enough" mentality. While I have no problem giving subcontractors time to learn the specific skills needed for their work with me, I simply have no interest in training (or retaining) someone who doesn't care enough to put their best into a project.

Here's a truncated but good basic checklist of the qualities for a successful employee or business owner:[7]

- They deem their work ethic as important as their paycheque.
- They are dependable, self-motivated and possess drive, energy and enthusiasm.
- They know how to work in a team.
- They are good at managing their time.
- They give their all to the task before them.
- They are punctual, love to learn, are trainable, flexible and creative.

LESSONS I'VE LEARNED

- Creativity is no excuse for headlong but ill-thought-out and inadequately prepared action.
- It's too easy to compromise quality in the need to take any and all jobs that will generate revenue.
- When building a team, be thorough when conducting due diligence and checking references. Resumes don't always tell the whole story.
- When building a team, hire people with strong skills in areas where you are weaker and those with personality strengths that complement your real or perceived weaknesses.
- Have someone hold you accountable for negative comments about yourself or about others; no excuses permitted.
- Form the habit of thinking and speaking positive words.
- Failing to get enough sleep or to eat properly will automatically produce negativity and a cranky attitude.

---

[7] Adapted from *What Color is Your Parachute*, 2012

- An attitude of thanksgiving is the greatest deterrent to discouragement. Reading inspirational books, including the Bible, on a daily basis helps me voice my praise.
- Displaying thankfulness might begin as an act of the will rather than an emotion of the heart, but keep practicing—the former will turn into the latter!
- Although Canadian, I do not have to apologize for all the sins of every person, corporation, or company in my beloved country; looking after my own will take up enough time, thank you.

Something to Think About

Media messages, book titles, and motivational presentations encouraging us to believe in ourselves and our abilities are everywhere. While a healthy dose of self-confidence can make the difference between success and failure, negative attitudes are probably more powerful.

I am personally acquainted with two examples of businesses that failed. Both were bookstores, though in two different communities. Admittedly, bookstores are a difficult sell at the best of times, simply because the print industry has been hit hard by competition from online and electronic options, but the launch of both stores created excitement in their respective areas. Finally, it seemed, residents would be able to browse for their favourite book or read while enjoying coffee and fresh baking. Sadly, both failed. While competition and a weak economy certainly played a role, many people felt that the owners of both stores displayed negative attitudes that drove customers away. They rarely smiled and they seemed unable or unwilling to engage their customers in friendly conversation. Their revenue stream dried up; customer traffic dwindled to almost nothing. While it's impossible to say the businesses would have succeeded under new management, the owners' less than congenial attitudes were definitely factors.

In contrast, a small bookstore and coffee shop was launched in our community of Powell River, BC, in the spring of 2005. I distinctly recall a Saturday morning just weeks after it opened. The main street was lined with people waiting for our annual Sea Fair parade to begin. To everyone's delighted surprise, Sean, the owner of the new bookstore, bounded down the sidewalk, took orders for drinks and goodies from the coffee shop and in an amazingly short time returned to serve his customers. Breakwater Books continues to be one of the more popular venues in our city for social gatherings and business meetings. In my estimation, the consistent atmosphere of congeniality and positive attitudes in the owners and employees plays a huge role in its success.

Adopting a positive attitude and determining to become genuinely thankful goes a long way toward boosting your own spirits and influencing those around you.

HERE ARE A FEW HINTS:

- When negative thoughts arise (and they will!) determine to harness their energy for something worthwhile. Go for a walk—that's good for the mind and body.
- Decide how you can turn an unjustified attack from someone into an opportunity to learn something positive.
- Create a thanksgiving list or journal that is dedicated to noting things for which to be grateful. These can include giving thanks for things as commonplace as clean sheets, a good cup of coffee, or the ability to see the beauty of a freshly mown lawn.
- When you focus on gratitude, your attitude will begin to change and that, in turn, affects those around you,

including those who might be looking for the skills and services you provide.

- Become conscious of negative thinking and immediately go to work replacing those thoughts with positive ones. No one said it would be easy, but it's vital to your personal and business success.
- Tell a trusted friend of your desire to overcome negativity and let them know that their willingness to hold you accountable would be appreciated.
- Set time aside each day to read words that will cultivate thanksgiving and provide you with plenty of "gratitude starters."

5 Keep Your Eye on the Goal

"Don't place mistakes on your head, their weight may crush you. Instead, place them under your feet and use them as a platform to view your horizons."[8]

John Gormley, Canadian lawyer and talk show host, interviewed and wrote about then Saskatchewan Roughriders head coach Kent Austin. In his comments, Gormley noted the "Austinisms" that guided Kent in moving himself and the football team forward.

Because these principles apply to every successful endeavour, I asked for and received permission to adapt them and pass them on to you:

- Be prepared: more than anything else, preparation is what is important.
- Care at a level that honours the position you're given to play (or the business you've invested in or the company you work for). Caring also extends to the people you work with, the clients you serve, and the people you hire.

[8] Posted on Facebook,www.spirituallyspeakingblogspot.com

- Recognize that success is going to cost you something. Be it finances, time, energy, or a host of other factors, everything worthwhile comes with a cost.
- Come to grips with the need to be accountable. Anyone who has believed in you or invested in you needs to know that you are upright in your dealings and accountable in your actions. That includes, among others, your banker, your customers, your suppliers and, above all, your family.
- Consider others in your dealings. Whether you are the sole proprietor and employee of your company or the head of a team of workers, caring about others sets you apart from the pack and reaps rewards of its own. It's also the mark of a true leader—in any and every area of life or business.
- Strive for excellence in everything you do. That, Kent says, doesn't just apply to the sports field; it means being the best husband or wife, best father or mother, best friend, best teammate and best employee or employer you can be.
- You must have a shared vision, a set of defined goals, and an underlying foundation of values. This is where a solid business plan and vision and mission statements become essential, because in the stresses that always come with growth, it's far too easy to lose sight of core purposes.
- Guard your integrity and your beliefs with your life. Not everyone is going to agree with you all the time, not even those you value most. Referring to the football field, other players in your "game" will be in different positions and moving at different speeds, but no matter what anyone else does (or doesn't do), don't sacrifice the things that matter most to you.

- Don't make excuses, and own up to your mistakes. What more needs to be said on that?
- Keep tabs on your feelings. Good days come, bad days come, and each brings its own set of emotions. Learning to control an emotional rollercoaster isn't easy but is essential in moving forward.
- View setbacks and seeming failures as stepping stones to future victories. Mary Peckford (1895–1979), actress and co-founder of United Artists, wrote this: "If you have made mistakes, there is always another chance for you. You may have a fresh start any moment you choose for this thing we call 'failure' is not the falling down but the staying down."
- Get rid of any attitude of entitlement. Austin says this: "I don't believe we 'should have' won a game we lost. You 'could' win a game. If you don't make enough of the right plays, then you 'shouldn't' have won it."[9]

Great advice, Kent! Thanks, John!

LESSON'S I'VE LEARNED THROUGH THIS PROCESS

- Nothing is more important than relationships. Be it your spouse, partner, child, trusted friend, grandparent or any number of others, make it a priority to love and communicate with them. There will always be work to do but they won't be here forever.
- Riches can be defined in more than monetary values.
- Live between the extremes of overworking to be rich and harbouring the soul of a miser.
- Keeping focused on a goal isn't as easy in reality as it is in theory. Stuff happens and rabbit trails abound.

---

[9] Gormley, John, *Austin Writes the Book on Team Building,* Saskatoon Star Phoenix Friday, November 30, 2007. Used by permission

- Focusing on goals can take on new meaning if it involves the "discovery" of transferrable skills or new opportunities that can lead to an increase in what you or your company can offer.
- Forced concentration has its role but sometimes it's necessary to step away from everything for a day—or a week.
- Don't neglect to spend time with a trusted mentor or friend. An hour for coffee together can work wonders.

SOMETHING TO THINK ABOUT

How do I want to be remembered when my life is ended?

6 Take Care of Yourself

"Get some rest. If you haven't got your health, you haven't got anything."

—*The Princess Bride*

"When you have your health, you have everything. When you do not have your health, nothing else matters at all."

—*Augusten Burroughs*

If there is one area in which I failed miserably, it is here. By allowing my work to consume my life, I created problems ranging from high blood pressure and some loss of vision to far too many hospital stays for pre-existing conditions. I've learned my lesson and now enjoy a much more relaxed and productive personal and business life. Having said that, I continue to pay for those first ten years of unrelenting stress. Maintaining good health, in every sense of the word, is not selfish. It's wise and it's necessary.

Physical Health:

To say stress plays havoc with our bodies is an understatement of immeasurable proportions. Risks associated with chronic stress include, but are certainly not limited to:

- Emotional exhaustion
- Heart disease
- Type 2 diabetes
- Metabolic syndrome
- Common cold
- Lower levels of mental health[10]

Because this book is directed to those who are in the age bracket of forty-five to sixty-four, there are health issues that rear their heads simply because we are getting older. As much as I hate to admit it, age is catching up with me. I was fifty-seven years old when I started my company; I'm now nearly seventy and my body demands an afternoon rest. There are a few other mandatory demands, but we won't go into those. It's important to recognize and respect limitations; if we don't, they will be imposed on us anyway but in a far more dramatic way.

Work-related health risks differ, of course, according to the job. Whether they are personal or work-related, or whether they involve the operation of heavy equipment, the constant impact of fingers on keyboards or anything in between, it's important to do everything within your power to mitigate those effects of your work on every aspect of your health.

EMOTIONAL HEALTH:

Emotions can be cruel taskmasters.

- Anger over being let go in spite of being a dependable employee, sometimes for years, has the power to breed internal bitterness and turmoil, and ultimately blur our focus for better things.

---

[10] M.S., E. (2010) Job Stress – The Effects and Management of Chronic Job Stress. [online] Available at: http://stress.about.com/od/stresshealth/a/job-stress.htm.

- Grief over lost opportunities and potential successes tends to suck out any sense of gratitude and envelopes us with an aura of miserable complaining.
- And who doesn't get discouraged when hours of "door knocking" turn into weeks or months of rejection?

I was often overwhelmed with grief at the loss of my former status, sorrow at what I perceived to be a future of uselessness, and anger at decisions that had left us financially vulnerable. No one will ever know the hours I would leave my desk, slip into a chair in the living room to weep my heart out, and then return to work on another assignment. My consolation was found in prayer, in reading of Scripture and in consciously committing our situation to God. However, that didn't mean I didn't experience times when I beat myself up out of frustration with the entire situation.

It seems it's when we've been dealt the harshest blows that we turn most violently upon ourselves or on those who are dearest to us. That's the time, however, when we most need to be gentle, to remind ourselves of the things that really matter.

The biggest step in my emotional healing was when I chose to turn my back on self-pity and begin moving forward with an "it's about time" attitude of appreciation for and to all those who had and continued to help me in my new career.

Social Health:

Wise man Solomon noted that to isolate oneself from the benefits of socializing and learning from others is to spurn wisdom. In other words, it's not only unwise, it's also unhealthy.[11]

---

[11] The Bible, Proverbs 18:1 (various translations)

Nurturing both long-term and newly made friendships provides an avenue of relaxation and encouragement that can be instrumental in reducing stress. That's good for the heart in more than one way. Here are just a few suggestions for boosting your social well-being:

- Don't neglect to frequent social events that have been part of your life. Sporting events, craft fairs, musical concerts, and church services are all examples.
- Consider joining a group that is new to you, or being the catalyst to begin a new group.
- Consider being part of the social activities of your business peer group—within your personal limits, of course. Also, tea or a meal with a co-worker after hours or on a day off can foster friendships that might never have formed within the work setting.
- There is no more effective way to meet other people, learn new things and gain perspectives that might otherwise never have been part of your life than to become a volunteer. Of course, it's important not to overextend yourself, but when carefully chosen and balanced with the rest of your life, volunteering can be one of the richest experiences of your life. How many men, women, and children (locally and globally) have been given a new chance at life because someone cared enough to give of their time and finances? How many pets have been rescued from abuse because volunteers intervened in their distress? How many homes have been built, heritage sites preserved, or sports, arts, and cultural activities supported through the efforts of volunteers? The answer to all these questions is simple: even if no one in your immediate world ever knows what you have contributed, every individual whose life has been

touched by your efforts will remember. Becoming part of the healing process itself brings health.

- In summary, keep active within your current circle of friends but don't neglect to add new friendships to your life.

MENTAL HEALTH:

Not to be forgotten is the need to respect and guard our mental health. The following tips were taken from the Canadian Mental Health Association, Richmond BC branch, website:[12]

Ten Tips for Mental Health

1. **Build Confidence** – Identify your abilities and weaknesses together, accept them, build on them and do the best with what you have.
2. **Accept Compliments** – Many of us have difficulty accepting kindness from others but we all need to remember the positive strokes when times get tough.
3. **Make Time for Family and Friends** – These relationships need to be nurtured; if taken for granted they will not be there to share life's joys and sorrows.
4. **Give and Accept Support** – Friends and family relationships thrive when they are "put to the test."
5. **Create a Meaningful Budget** – Financial problems cause stress. Over-spending on our "wants" instead of our "needs" is often the culprit.
6. **Volunteer** – Being involved in community gives a sense of purpose and satisfaction that paid work cannot.
7. **Manage Stress** – We all have stressors in our lives, but learning how to deal with them when they threaten to overwhelm us will maintain our mental health.

---

[12] Vcn.bc.ca (n.d.) Ten Tips for Mental Health. [online] Available at: http://www.vcn.bc.ca/rmdcmha/tips.html. Used by permission of CMHA, National/ACSM, nationale

8. **Find Strength in Numbers** – Sharing a problem with others who have had similar experiences may help you find a solution and will make you feel less isolated.
9. **Identify and Deal with Moods** – We all need to find safe and constructive ways to express our feelings of anger, sadness, joy and fear.
10. **Learn To Be At Peace with Yourself** – Get to know who you are, what makes you really happy, and learn to balance what you can and cannot change about yourself.

SPIRITUAL HEALTH:

This aspect of health is not listed last because it is least important, but because maintaining spiritual health is key to inner health and, ultimately, to the well-being of our minds and our bodies. Here are a few basic keys to maintaining spiritual health:

- Whatever your faith, cultivate a personal relationship with God and maintain regular and meaningful interaction with other members of your faith community. Whatever your choice of places to worship, be faithful in attending. They need you, but just as importantly, you need them.
- If you do not belong to any faith group or community, cultivate the habit of reading uplifting material or of serving others through non-profit organizations. In other words, don't neglect this vital part of your being.
- The process of changing careers guarantees that our minds will be crammed with information. There is no surer way to develop spiritual anemia than to omit reading scripture and/or other uplifting books. Make a point to take in spiritual food on a daily basis. You may not have an hour, but fifteen minutes is vastly superior to no time at all.

- Make a point of encouraging someone else. Be it through a handwritten note, a phone call, or an invitation to coffee or a meal, blessing someone else guarantees an eternal return on that investment.
- Being faithful means giving on a regular basis. Giving financial gifts to your local church, temple, or congregation as well as to national and global humanitarian organizations is not only a means of saying thanks for the good things we enjoy, it is conducive to your own inner health. As financially stressed as we may be, we're wealthy compared to the much of the world.
- When it comes to unkind words, unjust accusations, or unfair dealings, keep short accounts. What happened may not be fair, but who ever said life would be? To not forgive is to inflict yourself with spiritual cancer.

LESSONS I'VE LEARNED

- A monthly visit to a skilled therapeutic massage therapist is an important part of dealing with the physical stress created by the hours I spend typing.
- When I least want to communicate with friends or family, that's probably one of the times I need them the most.
- Respecting my body and its needs is an act of worship; failure to do so is to spurn my care of "the temple" I have been given.
- I can nearly always link sleeplessness, irritability, and discouragement to overwork.
- When sleepless nights plagued me, especially in the early days of my new business, I would try to turn them into times of prayer and praise or productive planning sessions. When that didn't work, I occasionally took a couple of over-the-counter sleep aids with a cup of hot milk.

- Mental, emotional, and spiritual health are too vital to overlook.
- "Lose weight" or "go for a long walk today" appear too frequently in my journal.

SOMETHING TO THINK ABOUT

If you don't already keep a journal, it might be a good idea to start. Each person needs to develop his or her individual style, so technique isn't as important as building the habit of expressing thoughts and noting events along the journey.

In order to resource significant items later on, I draw a picture of a book beside something I record as having gleaned from my reading. A roughly drawn pair of hands (a writer I am, an artist, not!) indicates a prayer request or an answer; other handwritten notes draw my attention when I re-read the journal.

About once a year, go back and review your entries; you may have forgotten some of the valuable lessons you learned, wisdom you gleaned, or people who were there for you during a particularly tough time. You may even want to send a thank-you note to those people—they may be the ones needing a bit of encouragement right then.

For years I poured my heart out through ink-blood; now, looking back at those volumes, I am astounded at how far I have come, how much I have learned and, just as significant, that I still struggle with some of the same things that have challenged me for decades.

One other thing: If you suffer from prolonged sleeplessness or insomnia, check with your doctor.

SECTION 2

Developing Your Plan

7 Creating Your Plans

"Planning is bringing the future into the present so that you can do something about it now."

—Allan Lakein

A: If You're Looking for Employment

A lot has changed since we middle-agers graduated from high school! Among those changes are the ways in which employers look for candidates and employees look for jobs. Networking and "who you know" are increasingly important factors and technology has reinvented the job search and hiring process. For example, a diminishing number of employers use classified ads to post jobs, relying instead on word of mouth and/or online postings.

If you are opting to seek employment rather than start your own business, here are a few tips.[13]

Resume Preparation:

- Make sure your resume is tailored to the job you're seeking. If you want a job as a financial advisor, avoid emphasizing your experience as a chef.

[13] Adapted from and used by permission of Career Link, Powell River, BC

- Have your mentor and/or trusted friend review your resume. Ask them to give you honest feedback as to its suitability to the position you're seeking. Ask them or someone else who is skilled in editing to check your resume for spelling or grammatical errors.
- Don't count classified ads as your sole resource. Check your telephone book or do online research to find companies or businesses within your area of expertise who would be prospective employers.
- Call or visit these prospective employers. When I moved from one province to another after three years in business, I basically had to start over again. One of the first things I did was prepare copies of my portfolio, source contact information for every company in our city I thought might be interested in contracting my service, and then visited each of them. It took me weeks, and yielded no results but certainly got my name into the business community, and drove me to more prayer. It was good for spiritual health, not so good for the bank account. Like seeds planted in the ground, however, those efforts eventually grew to pay great dividends.
- When applying for a job and especially if you're granted an interview, take time to find out all you can about that company. Expand your knowledge of the product or service it offers, its mission and vision statement, an overview of its clients and how you see yourself fitting into the corporate or company environment.

B: If You're Planning to Open Your Own Business

"If you fail to prepare then you are preparing to fail."

—Benjamin Franklin

You've had time to think, but now it's time to begin some solid planning. You now recognize your traits, skills and abilities more clearly, you've identified the direction you want to take, and you've already begun the process of taking action. I offer you my genuine congratulations, because those in themselves are huge and often emotionally stressful decisions. You've proven that you're serious in your commitment to your new role and you know what you're aiming for. Simply put, you are preparing to succeed.

A friend and business colleague, Don, taught me one of the most valuable lessons I learned in starting my company: learn to take baby steps. I've mentioned this principle before and I'll mention it again, because it's worth repeating and particularly useful as you move forward in the planning process. Another highly successful professional writer kindly allowed me to adapt her advice for those running their own businesses.

Begin with TETE, the French word for "head"[14]

Time:

Time is life's most precious commodity and the one most easily wasted. In planning, take careful consideration of time and how it applies to every aspect of your life.

Begin by determining how much time it takes to perform tasks related to your new career or job. For example:

- How long will it take you to create a product or service you're going to put on the market?
- How much time will you need to conduct interviews, do research, or write an article? How much time do you need to build, prepare, or source supplies for that service or product?
- If you're opening a retail outlet, how many hours per day/week do you plan to spend at the business?

14 O'Leary, Denyse, *Surviving and Succeeding as a Freelance Writer,* self-published, p. 3. Used by permission.

- How much time are you prepared to spend in marketing yourself, contacting prospective clients, and conducting research?

These are just a few of many questions to ask as you parcel out the hours of each day. Neglecting to plan for wise use of time is the best way to ensure failure in most every aspect of life.

Take advantage of software programs to assist you in your planning. Although there are many on the market, check out the free online options. Unless you need highly complex features, you can save hundreds of dollars this way. One of my favourites is Freemind™, a simple time-mapping program.

One of the programs I purchased and downloaded is TraxTime™, which allows me to track time spent on projects and thus provide clients with a detailed breakdown of hours billed on invoices. I've used this program since I launched my business more than a decade ago and I count it one of my most valuable tools.

Freemind is, as the name suggests, available at no cost and last time I checked the basic Traxtime program was still the same price as I paid in 2000.

Energy:

Learning how to respect my body's energy level has been the most difficult challenge for me; it may be for you, as well. In fact, guarding my strength for the most important things is an ongoing fight. Here are a few suggestions:

- Decide on a schedule; that probably means choosing what you will have to give up in order to reach your goals.
- Volunteer wisely; needs are everywhere but no one person can meet them all.
- Allow yourself time to have a life. Life-work balance is essential to maintain all areas of your health.

- Get enough rest, eat properly, and include physical exercise in your plan.
- Schedule your days to maximize your peak performance times. For me it's the morning, but determine what works best for you.

Training:

The original Mentor is a character from Homer's epic poem, *The Odyssey*. When Odysseus, King of Othaca, went to fight in the Trojan War, he entrusted the care of his kingdom and the oversight of his son, Telmachus, to a trusted servant named Mentor.

Just as Mentor poured his energies into training Temachus, the value of a trusted mentor cannot be overestimated. Here are a few points from a workshop I give on the topic:

A mentor is someone who comes alongside to provide:

- Knowledge
- Insight
- Perspective
- Wisdom
- Encouragement
- The ability to see clearly

The process of changing careers is not easy and I can think of no more valuable resource than linking up with a mentor who is willing to provide advice and guidance in your journey. I was blessed to have three experienced businessmen act as mentors for me; without the knowledge they imparted and the encouragement they provided, I would not have acquired the skills I now possess.

Here are some things to consider in your quest to find your mentor:

- Mentors do not typically come to you; you need to seek out someone you admire, who has the appropriate work or life experience from which you can learn, and—most importantly—someone you can trust.
- Conversely, you must be willing to learn, willing to be corrected, sensitive to the fact that a mentor is not on duty 24/7, and most importantly, trustworthy.
- Talk to someone in your community or network who has changed career paths and get their advice on how to begin.
- Go to the local library or employment resource centre for reading material.
- Be sure to check out community and government-funded agencies offering employment resource training or services. In addition to the excellent training programs available, clients typically have the use of computers and printer for resumes, Internet access for job and career information, an online database of employers, daily updated job postings, a job/career resource library, community or educational services and access to fax, photocopier, newspapers and telephone. While there are many Canadian and US sites that list available services in both countries, several key addresses are listed below.[15] Online, join professional networking sites such as LinkedIn.
- Learning isn't all academic in nature. Never stop learning about subjects such as etiquette, public speaking, or gracious hospitality.
- Don't restrict your learning to one medium; there's lots of valuable information from the print media as well as the world wide web.

---

[15] www.jobbank.gc.ca; www.youremploymentservices.ca; www.dol.gov/dol/location.html

- Don't forget to tap into the knowledge and wisdom that comes from speaking with those who have already travelled this path.
- Learn from observation; watch and emulate those you most admire. For approximately fifteen years, I've written a weekly inspirational column for a number of newspapers. The question I am asked most often is this: "Where do you get all the ideas for your columns?" My answer is simple: I have learned to carefully observe what's going on around me.
- No matter what area of interest you are pursuing, it's important to learn from others. Watch how your competitors market their products or service. Listen to ads and, even more importantly, listen to how consumers describe their experiences with various companies. If they're not happy, find out why; if they are, it's even more important to find out what your competition is doing right.
- Learn from published articles and studies. What consumer trends have a direct impact on your work?
- Gaining information from social media and online articles is no longer an option, it's a given.

Learn to plan in stages because careers, like life, are organic. The first step was in understanding yourself and your needs. The second involves visualizing your future and your goals. The third, transcribing your ideas into a written plan.

Equipment and Resources:

THINGS:

Since every situation differs, it is impossible to list all the types of equipment required for your new career. A good rule of thumb for me has been asking will purchasing this really add value to my company? Will my health be improved by the purchase of this item or items? How soon will this purchase provide a return on my investment? In summary, you need good equipment, but perhaps not now, and not necessarily with the latest bells and whistles.

PEOPLE:

Another friend and mentor, Ken, instilled in me the confidence that I could succeed with my company despite my lack of formal education. Although I continue to learn on the job and from training opportunities, Ken gave me wise counsel when he told me to surround myself with people who know more than I do. I attribute much of my success and many of my projects that came about because I paid attention to this counsel. I'm passing on some practical ideas on the subject:

- Don't hang out with those people who always and only know that it can't be done.
- Choose close friends and business colleagues who will not only support and encourage you but will challenge you to grow.
- Be selective about those you choose as closest friends. This isn't about being snobby or neglecting people who need a helping hand up, it's about protecting your character and your reputation (there is a difference between those two). If you think those things don't matter, you probably haven't read the newspapers or business publications lately.
- It's important to hire subcontractors or employees who will enhance the strength of your company's services or products and bolster the areas in which you are not as strong or knowledgeable. Because I have had the privilege of working with a financial advisor, I am able to offer

expanded report services to clients; I collect research data, my colleague crunches the numbers, and together we analyze the results and write reports.

C: WRITING YOUR BUSINESS PLAN

I will not attempt to detail all the work that goes into creating a business plan; others have written on the subject. The following is a basic template and one I've used to guide my business as well as in helping others to prepare strategic plans for their emerging businesses. Hint: don't forget to look back at the roadmap you created in Chapter Three.

Business Overview

- Business History
- Mission Statement
- Vision Statement
- Objectives
- Ownership
- Location and Facilities

Products and Services

- Description of Products or Services
- Key Features of Products or Services
- Production of Products or Services
- What sets your Products or Services apart from the competition?

Industry Overview

- What is my target market?
- How large is that market?
- Who is my competition?

Marketing Strategy

- Pricing strategy
- Promotion strategy
- How will this company meet and beat the competition?
- Strategic plans if targeting a niche market?

Management and Staffing

- Hiring criteria
- Regulatory issues
- Local bylaws
- Provincial/State regulations
- Federal regulations
- Employment/insurance/union issues

Financial Plan[16]

- Starting balance sheet
- Forecast Income Statement
- Cash flow forecast

LESSONS I'VE LEARNED

- You usually get what you pay for and cheap can be the most costly.
- Value quality subcontractors and/or staff and let them know that in tangible ways.
- Access employment programs that provide financial incentives to hiring mature workers who have recently completed training courses.
- Regard time as an eternal commodity that if wasted cannot be recouped.
- Keeping the former statement in mind is the best way to spend time wisely.

[16] Appendix A: template samples for setting up budgets for a hypothetical company

- Never forget those who helped you and continue to help you along the way.
- Sit down each week, list commitments and responsibilities for the next seven days, and put them in order of priority.
- Make sure your priorities honour your spiritual life, nurture your relationships with family and friends, and meet your work-related commitments. Since it's probably impossible to do everything, pare the first list down again.
- Don't forget to celebrate! Since thirty percent of new businesses in Canada fail to make the five-year mark, I decided I'd let my world know that Words of Worth did. I took an entire year's advertising budget and used it to let my new business peers and colleagues know. I booked a room in a local hotel, ordered finger foods, and scoured the local discount stores for tablecloths and accessories in my company colours. I invited our mayor and town council (most of them attended) as well as other business owners I considered potential clients. The room was packed and the response, positive. One prominent and influential business owner remarked, "Why do we always forget to celebrate?" My next event is scheduled for 2013.

SOMETHING TO THINK ABOUT

If you haven't already done it, now is the time to sit down and begin writing that business plan; your new career is crying out for structure and form. Use your roadmap (see Chapter Two) and your banner (see Chapter Three) to get the process started.

8 Finding Clients

"The secret of success is to do common things uncommonly well."

—John D. Rockefeller

There are four grocery stores where I live. One belongs to a North American chain, one to a prominent Western Canadian group of companies, and one to a smaller but growing Vancouver Island-based company, and the other is one of the earliest independently owned stores. Each of them offers good product, good service, and unique differences.

For example, you can't beat the marinated steak sold at the store with its original wood floors still intact. Staff at the in-store butcher shop are both ready and qualified to give great cooking advice (I hear both the butchers are also chefs by training).

The store linked to the international chain boasts a pharmacy. I'd say it's rather handy to do the shopping while pharmacists dole out your prescription drugs. Talk about one-stop shopping.

It's the bulk shopping section that usually takes me to the provincially owned outlet. As just one of a number of stores owned by the chain in the parent group, it's changed names in the past several years. It's also changed a lot of other things in the process. That's the place I go to purchase the various seeds, nuts, and grains I use in baking bread and other goodies.

It's what is going on in the fourth store, however, that most intrigues me. In fact, this growing chain has marketing down to a science. For starters, there's a daily special advertised on a large digital board in front of the store. It's become customary for drivers to slow down or speed up, as necessary, to find out "what's on for today." Then, as if that wasn't enough, they've introduced an additional "Daily Special from 4pm-6pm only" that's advertised online and via a free cell phone app.

The latter establishment doesn't boast the lowest prices but it's easy to see that this store is growing. A genuine family atmosphere, shopping carts that don't require the customary twenty-five cents to unlock them from the row, a scanning program that provides the opportunity to receive an unadvertised reduction in price on random items, and the intrigue of never knowing the daily special until you drive past the store are powerful drawing cards. A common question in my everyday conversations goes like this: "What's on special at Quality Foods today?"

If you started your company in response to existing, pent-up demand for your products or services, rejoice! For most of us, the next step in getting a new business up and running is seeking out clients. Marketing is key and it's a science. Here are a few hints to help you get going on all the hard work that lies ahead.

GO BACK TO YOUR BUSINESS PLAN.

One of the great temptations when starting up a business is what I call "shooting blind." Because the need for revenue is a key factor, it's tempting to dilute products or services to attract clients rather than refining and honing your business to achieve its maximum value. I made the mistakes of taking on jobs that either paid a mere pittance for the hours of work they required, or stretched my resources beyond my level of experience. I thank God daily for those subcontractors who rose to the occasion and helped me out!

One of the functions of a business plan is to identify your target or niche market. As a writer I have learned that within the non-fiction genre there is much to consider, including but not limited to industry-specific terminology, differences in interview questions and approaches, "slants" on articles or research reports, and stylistic options.[17]

Distinguish your company in your marketplace by precisely defining what you do and who you want to reach out to as customers.

Establish prices that reflect fair value to you and your clients.

Establishing prices can be a challenge, especially in times of economic volatility. As corporations and companies downsize, laid-off employees are increasingly using their skills and expertise to launch their own consulting businesses. Perhaps that's what you're doing!

Establishing a fee structure carries pitfalls, particularly from either extreme: charging more than the market will bear or pricing your products and services so low that you lose credibility along with meaningful revenue.

Know what you want to say to the marketplace.

What do you want people to think of when they pick up

---

[17] Examples include: *The Canadian Press Stylebook* and *Wall Street Words* by David L. Scott

your business card, read your ad or hear your company name? Does your business name reflect the message you want to convey?

Consider using a tagline to clarify what you do or sell. I'd not considered that when I first chose my company's name, Words of Worth. I somehow assumed people would know that I was a writer and speaker. They didn't. After being asked on a number of occasions to explain exactly what I did and finding "I write and speak" to be a wholly unsatisfactory response, to them and to me, I sat down and condensed my thoughts. My business card now reads, "Words of Worth: *writing for and about business.*"

REVIEW, RESEARCH, AND CO-OPERATE.

Remember the work you put into researching your target market? Now it's time to expand the results of that research by tapping into the power of co-operation and co-marketing.

Let's use the example of writing again: I love to write and I've also developed strong research skills, but I don't do numbers. In fact, one of the first things I did when I launched Words of Worth was retain an accountant and I still count that as one of the smartest moves I've made in my career. I do know someone who specializes in economic development and financial planning, and by partnering our skills we've been awarded a number of great contracts.

A friend and her husband have launched a business making and selling salmon grilling planks made of pre-logged, local old growth Western Cedar. By packaging and stamping the product with the logo of another small manufacturer, the couple sells their planks to the manufacturer that then offers their customers unique but affordable thank-you gifts for their business.

Offer incentives.

I once offered to write a 350-word article as a donation to a silent auction table. The response was more than I expected and a well-established business now has me on their list of future contractors. It only cost a couple of hours' work, yet yielded more advertising than an expensive print media piece ever did.

Put legs to your words and keep your ear to the ground.

As brilliant as a marketing plan can be, the need for old-fashioned hard work isn't diminished. Depending on what your company offers, the work plan will differ but the need to dedicate time to building up clientele remains the same. Get on the phone to companies or individuals that match your market, respond to Requests for Proposal (RFPs) and Requests for Interest (RFIs), make daily checks of online employment ads, online sites advertising various levels of government RFPs and RFIs, and check print media. Visit your local employment offices.[18]

Since word of mouth still plays an important part in the awarding of many jobs or contracts, connecting with groups such as your Chamber of Commerce and industry-specific networking links often gives occasion to hear of upcoming work. You may still have to compete, but you won't lose the opportunity to be part of that competition.

Maintain a reputation for living and working with integrity.

While people notice when you live your personal and business life with integrity, they make more noise about you if

[18] One such site is www.bcbid.gov.bc.ca. This is for the Province of British Columbia, but check around for other city, municipality, state or provincial sites.

you fail to live up to what you proclaim as your scruples. Sadly we often hear of fraud, corruption, and unethical lifestyles and business practices, but to be known as one who is honest and upright in their dealings not only garners respect, it enhances a good night's sleep and attracts people looking for the services or products you offer.

THINGS I'VE LEARNED

- Don't give up. Persistence, coupled with a solid business plan and the product and services to go with it, does pay off.
- Remaining focused on your goals while consistently producing work on budget, on time, and as promised (or more) will eventually result in customers coming to you rather than you seeking them out.
- Besides competition, politics on any level can be a huge challenge. I choose to steer clear whenever possible.
- Steering clear of politics is rarely possible, so determine how you and your business will respond to issues. Establish your convictions but be open to hear both sides of the case.
- Always carry a good supply of business cards with you and make sure they're not creased or soiled.

SOMETHING TO THINK ABOUT

Above all, remember that your business is not about you, it's about "them," so be sure that the products or services your company will offer will meet the needs of your current and potential customers. What may seem perfectly rational and important to you may lack an element that results in clients heading elsewhere. It is never wasted time to find out what your particular market sector is looking for.

One of the first projects my company worked on was for a college on the Canadian prairies. At that time, Precision Agriculture, the marriage of traditional farming practices with GPS and GIS technology, was just emerging. This college had been in the process of determining if there would be interest in its offering a course in the subject.

Over the course of the next month I spoke with fifty equipment manufacturers, dealers and end-users/farmers. Data collected indicated there was interest in the proposed course, but it also highlighted specific areas of concern. Using this valuable information, the client was able to determine the level of interest from each sector as well as what factors were important to respondents. Though this was just part of the process, it was gratifying to see that the following school year this course was part of the curriculum.

To find out what your future clients are looking for, consider putting together a short survey. Ask questions pertinent to your company's offering using tools such as online surveys[19], social media, or personal contact. Here are several simple examples:

1) **If you were to choose my product/service, what would be the most important factor in that decision? Check all that apply.**

   Simple to use: __
   Environmentally friendly: __
   Easily accessible: __
   Availability of service: __
   Cost: __
   All of the above: __
   None of the above: __

[19] Some companies offer free online survey templates. Data is tallied automatically, making processing the results much quicker and easier.

2) **Why are you considering moving from your current product/service provider to another? Check all that apply.**

   Product/service not up to expected quality: —
   Cost of delivery of product or service: —
   Competitor offers better incentives/benefits: —
   Customer service was poor, unfriendly or unhelpful:—
   Current company never comes up with new ideas:—

While these are merely sample questions, use them to create others that hone in on what your current and future customers are looking for. Tally the collected data and put it into a graph or chart for maximum visual impact. Determine how you can improve your product or service or how you can create a fresh approach to what is already a top-quality offering.

9 Minding Your Money

"The only thing money gives you is the freedom of not worrying about money."

—Johnny Carson

When launching my business, I was exceptionally fortunate in that I did not have to invest in a lot of equipment, supplies, or furniture. In fact, my major purchases consisted of a new printer and toner, a desk and a ream of paper. Not everyone is so fortunate, though. Some businesses require a substantial layout of money in order to purchase equipment and supplies, rent office space, buy or lease a vehicle, obtain garage or warehouse facilities … and the list goes on.

The two scenarios couldn't be more different in creating a budget, but the same principle applies: make sure you carefully track your company's assets and liabilities, spend wisely and save regularly. Although there may be a number of reasons for the following statistic, it's wise to consider that approximately thirty percent of all new businesses in Canada do not survive five years. It can never hurt to budget wisely.

MAKE A WELL-THOUGHT-OUT BUDGET A PRIORITY IN YOUR BUSINESS PLANNING.

Starting a business is fraught with concerns, but let's face it, the thought of putting ourselves and our talents and skills into the marketplace is exciting. In fact, if it isn't, perhaps the idea needs to be reconsidered. Having said that, the enthusiasm over what you have to offer the world must not override foundational issues, including a working budget.

As I've emphasized throughout this book, bookkeeping and accounting definitely are not my strengths; what I do understand and practice is a commitment to living within my budget. Whatever your situation, it's important to develop a business budget. I've gleaned the following valuable information from online sources and business colleagues.[20]

STEPS IN PREPARING A BUSINESS BUDGET

Here's where the act of taking baby steps is once again the best advice to follow. Begin the process by listing all your business goals, including projected goals for the next five years or more. What do you want to achieve? What is involved in reaching those goals? What do you estimate it will cost to achieve each of those goals?

ONCE YOU'VE SET THOSE PROJECTED GOALS, LOOK AT WHAT DOCUMENTS YOU HAVE AT HAND.

This is where you need your income statement, your balance sheet, past income tax returns, and a projection of immediate and monthly cash flow. You'll also need to be thorough in listing any outstanding debts as well as liabilities and assets.

---

[20] Helpful websites include: Sample templates for creating financial statements http://www.vertex42.com/ExcelTemplates/business-startup-costs.html; Four Steps to Developing a Business Budget www.sitepoint.com/develop-a-business-budget/

NEXT COME THE COLD HARD FACTS: YOU NEED TO DETERMINE HOW MUCH IT'S GOING TO COST TO REACH YOUR GOALS.

Dealing with one goal at a time, determine the specific costs associated with reaching that goal. How much will you have to spend to acquire that new piece of equipment? The larger office space? More staff? How much will you need to pay out for business licences, membership dues and taxes? Once you've worked out the annual cost, break it down month by month. Do this for every item on your list of goals.

CREATE THE BUDGET.

Armed with the work you've done in those first three steps, it's time to develop a spreadsheet. See Appendix A for budgeting template samples created by an accountant who has worked extensively with owners of start-up businesses.

RE-EVALUATE ON A REGULAR BASIS.

No matter how far along in the process, wisdom dictates that you regularly assess where you are in this journey. Perhaps a five-year goal now appears doable in four years or, conversely, that new equipment you planned on buying next month might need to be postponed until finances are in place. Re-evaluating is not defeat; it's reality-based wisdom.

LESSONS I'VE LEARNED

- Make sure you have a solid financial plan.
- Set up a budget and be diligent in keeping track of what you spend vs. what you earn.
- Keep track of *every* expense and keep *every* receipt. Pay no bills and write no cheques without proper documentation, i.e. a sales slip or an invoice.

- I put all my expenses on a credit card in order to gain bonus points that can be used for travel.
- Never put anything on a credit card that you cannot pay, in full, when the next statement comes in.
- I was fortunate in that I had to purchase very little office furniture, supplies or equipment, though I certainly was tempted to upgrade when it wasn't really necessary.
- Know what saves you money and what costs money. Don't forget to factor in wasted time and resources. Sometimes "more expensive" actually saves money in the long run—but not always. Paper is expensive, so consider recycling paper for printing internal documents.
- Sometimes it's necessary to spend money in order to make money. Get high-quality business cards, stationery letterhead, advertising, etc.
- Unless it's essential, don't waste money on the latest equipment or furniture—that can always come later.
- Think ahead and put money aside each month for year-end taxes, membership dues (Chamber of Commerce, etc.), ongoing training, etc.
- Find a reputable accountant—it's well worth the cost to know that this person is up to date on provincial/state or federal regulations and that sales and income tax charges have been accurately calculated and reported.

SOMETHING TO THINK ABOUT

Whether you're looking after your own financial affairs or you've hired a bookkeeper or accountant, it's essential to understand financial trends.

If you're not in the habit of doing this, now is a good time to begin. Using your financial records for the past twelve months, ask yourself these questions:

- Are my sales up, down, or flat, year to year? Why?
- What factors have influenced that trend and are they factors within my company's control?
- Is a particular aspect of my business doing better than another? Worse? Why?
- Are there things I can do to reverse a negative trend, boost flat sales, or continue an upward trend in revenue generation?

Write yourself a report based on the answers to those questions and begin looking for innovative answers.

10 Communication and Networking

"Say what you mean, and mean what you say, but don't say it mean!"

—Author Unknown

COMMUNICATION

The importance of communication cannot be overemphasized. In every area of life, including the world of business, failure to communicate in a timely and effective manner can make the difference between success and failure. Whether the medium is fax, telephone, cell phone, letter, website or social media software, keep the lines of communication open. Communication is the open door to effective networking, spreading of ideas, and promotion of your new career or enterprise.

I admit that poor communication is one of things that most annoys me. Failure to respond to messages can cause misunderstanding, lost opportunities, or a false sense that you and/or your business simply don't care. With the explosion of social media websites, it takes very little time for news to get out that you failed to keep your word or show up for a promised appointment.

EMAIL GUIDELINES

Be well informed regarding email etiquette. There is much information on this topic online, but here are a few hints to start with:

- Make sure your emails open and close with a courteous greeting.
- Unless you're corresponding with someone you know well, be sure to use the proper amount of respect, including the correct spelling of names, to approach recipients.
- Don't "Reply to all" or forward emails unless it is appropriate. Flooding inboxes with irrelevant emails is annoying to say the least. I run into this all the time, where a casually worded email intended for a single colleague ends up with a customer or client. Depending on the content, it can come off as unprofessional, or worse—it can harm your reputation.
- Save your time and that of email recipients by putting the purpose of your message in the Subject line.[21]

RESPONDING TO REQUESTS FOR INFORMATION

Even if you don't have the answers at your fingertips, at least let the person know that you are working on providing a response. Acknowledge the effort they made in getting in touch with you and then get back to them as soon as possible.

RESPONDING TO FORMAL BUSINESS OR SOCIAL INVITATIONS

RSVP, or *responder s'il vous plait*, implies a reply is requested. The French phrase often appears on wedding and other

---

[21] Jeff Mowatt, BComm, CSP, Customer Service Strategist, Certified Professional Speaker

invitations, but it is similarly important to respond to business-related social events.

Margaret Page, Professional Life Coach, Business Coach and Vancouver-etiquette expert, writes: [22]

"Always respond to your host, and if you cancel, do so verbally (no emails or phone messages please) and promptly reschedule."

With Margaret's gracious permission, I'm sharing her Networking Nuggets with you:[23]

- When you meet people at a networking event, shake hands, smile and look them in the eye. Greeting people warmly is always welcome.
- Have professionally designed and printed business cards available to give on request. Better yet, make a point of asking others for their cards. That way you can follow up and not wait for them to contact you.
- Listen well when talking with others. Use your eyes, heart and brain as well as your ears to engage in a full conversation. Never look over the person's shoulder to pick out someone "more important."
- Take opportunities to praise people for the contributions they make. Letting them take a bow makes you both feel good!
- Make a point of regularly connecting with people on your key contact list, even when you aren't requesting anything from them. They will feel nurtured by your outreach.
- Follow up your networking conversations within a day or two (that's why you ask for the other person's business card). Graciously follow through on any agreements you make and do it as soon as practical.

---

[22] Page, *Cognito*, Etiquette Page Enterprises, see www.etiquettepage.com

[23] Page, *Page's Nine Nuggets for Networking*. Used with permission.

- If you're in a conversation with people who are badmouthing others, do the reverse. Say positive things instead: "good mouth" them. (Quote attributed to Susan Rhohan)
- Acknowledge what others do and who they are by sending cards, emails or letters. Frequently congratulate those in your networking circle on their ideas and achievements.
- Always ask people how you can help them accomplish their goals. Get specific details and follow through on what you have promised. Doing that will build loyalty and trust every time!

MARKET YOURSELF

Stay focused.

In those first tentative years in business, Ron, a friend and mentor, taught me invaluable research skills. It's only because of his commitment to my success that I developed the skills and confidence to take the next step. Three years after that initial launch of Words of Worth, my husband and I moved from an agricultural, prairie-based environment to a geographically isolated community on the west coast of British Columbia. This move forced me to refocus my attention from mega agriculture to tiny, organic farms. Not only did I struggle with geographic claustrophobia, I now found myself without a focus. I'd like to forget those first several years of adjustment, but I dare not because they were key to my business growing to where it is today.

Once you've decided the route you want to take and you've initiated the first positive steps, it's time to seek out services available in your community or business network. Here is a partial list of such resources; you'll likely think of or know others unique to your locale:

- Local newspapers
- Community leaders
- Government-funded agencies
- Business Network International
- Chamber of Commerce
- Toastmasters
- Social media such as Facebook and LinkedIn
- Individual business owners

Probably the best advice I received after launching my business came from a friend and mentor. I've mentioned it before and it bears repeating: "Surround yourself with people who know more than you do." I took that advice and never looked back. Over the past years I purposefully took opportunities to meet successful business owners and associate myself with organizations, individuals, and publications with resources relevant to my company. Now, when interviewing and hiring subcontractors, I attempt to assess their compatibility with my skills and abilities as thoroughly as their education and experience. It took several bad experiences to learn that what appears on a person's resume is just part of the picture.

Newspapers

Fortunately for me, my first steps in networking proved to be pivotal in the success of my company. Shortly after we arrived in BC, I read a notice in our weekly newspaper concerning changes to home-based business by-laws. I attended a local meeting and met the manager of our newly launched economic development office. The bulk of my early success in our community came about as a result of attending the meeting rather than reading about it in next week's paper. Here's why:

In a conversation following the by-law meeting, I learned that the manager of that new economic development office had moved with his family the same week we did. He'd also lived on the prairies and recalled reading an agriculture study I'd written. As a result of our conversation, we became business associates. Over the years since that meeting, we've researched and prepared a number of reports for government, non-profit, and business clients.

Learn to ask lots of appropriate questions.

One of the things I most enjoy in my work as a freelance writer is interviewing and writing about successful business owners and/or managers. I regularly ask questions like this: Are you the founder of this company? What led you into this particular field? What were or are your greatest challenges? What are your greatest sources of satisfaction? If you had something you could do over, what would it be?

It's more than interesting to hear their answers. One in particular stands out. A professional consultant shut down his business in the downtown of a major city and opened a small engine repair shop in an outlying area. When asked why, he responded without hesitation: "Because of traffic congestion heading in and out of the city."

You're probably reading this because you have changed careers or are contemplating a change to possibly open your own business. The old maxim about not needing to re-invent the wheel holds true. Asking lots of questions will enable you to learn from others, take note of the challenges they've faced, and plan accordingly.

Link up with organizations dedicated to helping business people succeed.

Linking up with our local Business Networking International (BNI™) chapter proved to be another door-opener.[24] A professional marketing organization, BNI specializes in its members giving and receiving word-of-mouth referrals. Part of each member's commitment is to carry business cards for every other member. When a 'prospect' is met, the business card and testimonial information is shared and a referral most often created.[25]

Since membership is limited to one business per category per chapter, competition for a referral in any one category is eliminated.

This is just one off-line organization dedicated to generating leads for member businesses, so seek out what other local or online groups might meet your needs. Take into consideration membership fees when deciding what suits you best. Since there are no guarantees and membership fees are relatively expensive, realize that you are taking a gamble on results … but the return on your investment (ROI) could be well worth the cost.

Chamber of Commerce

The benefits of a Chamber of Commerce membership usually include unique networking opportunities, low rates for some credit cards, discounts on banking, health and group insurance plans, and discounts for long distance and cell phone service, hotel rates, and specified retail outlets.

While a lot of networking opportunities do not involve a layout of cash, membership in both BNI and the Chamber of Commerce costs money. I have found, however, that interest received on those investments far exceeded the risk. Whatever the programs offered by your local chapter, be they regular meetings, luncheons, social activities, community service events, or involvement at a board level, you benefit

[24] Check out www.bnicanada.ca. Latest figures on the website state that there are more than 145,000 members worldwide.

[25] www.bnicanada.ca. About Page

in direct proportion to your commitment and your level of participation.

Strategic networking provides opportunities that might otherwise be missed. As I interacted with my new colleagues, I became aware of valuable resources through government-funded organizations such as Career Link and Community Futures[26]. Because I did not qualify for employment insurance, I could not access all the benefits, but better to take what is available rather than lamenting over what is not. I have gleaned support and wise counsel from programs through both those agencies. Not only that, I have benefited greatly by hiring a number of graduates from these programs. Seeking out government-funded resource programs is about receiving a hand-up rather than viewing them as a hand-out.

Toastmasters[27]

I count joining a local Toastmasters club as one of the best decisions I've made since launching my business. Not only have I honed my public speaking skills, I've learned how to minimize distracting gestures and speech patterns, gained a new sense of confidence in presenting material, and acquired a wonderful new circle of friends and colleagues.

Other Business Owners

Make it a habit to get together for coffee or a meal with other business owners. Remove "talking shop" from the agenda and make it strictly a relaxing social meeting. It's amazing how much you can absorb and how many opportunities will open just by becoming friends. Even more importantly, it's good for your mental health.

---

[26] These types of services may go by another name. Check your provincial or state employment offices.

[27] www.toastmasters.org

THINGS I'VE LEARNED THROUGH THIS PROCESS

- "NETWORKING is the single most powerful marketing tactic to accelerate and sustain success for any individual or organization!"[28]
- Develop a strong network of business connections.
- Become involved in networking groups; if none exists, start one.
- Always be looking for business and/or employment opportunities.
- If you're a business owner, always be on the alert for potential team members or other independent contractors with whom you might partner on a project. Surround yourselves with people who know more than you do!
- No matter what the personal cost, always do everything within your power to keep your word, pay your share of lunches out, avoid compromising situations or business deals, and above all, guard your personal integrity.

SOMETHING TO THINK ABOUT

- Keep a positive attitude. Decide what you have to offer an employer or customer and don't be afraid to "sell" those skills and qualities. Write a thirty-second "elevator speech" that describes what your business offers its clients. Practice it on friends and family and, most importantly, keep it brief but power-packed!
- Be willing to step outside your comfort zone; use some audacity! On the other hand, be sure you don't promise what you can't produce.

---

[28] Adam H. Small currently serves as the CEO of Strategic Business Network, LLC., which he founded in 2004. While managing SBN's growth, Adam pursues additional entrepreneurial activities as both an active investor and business partner in several enterprises including: Synchevents, Thread F/X, Inc., Nashville Bank & Trust and Essent Healthcare.

- Personal hygiene: be squeaky clean and professionally dressed for every social or business meeting or appointment; all the qualifications in the world won't counter-balance the impression made by unpleasant body odour, bad breath, or inappropriate or untidy apparel.

11 Innovation – Setting Yourself Apart

"Innovation is not a luxury."

—*Robert F. Brands*[29]

Gerry Merten, owner of Scotland-based Paragon Inks, knows all about the power of innovation. After hitting a financial low spot, he realized things had to change. In an article that appeared in *The Costco Connection*, Merten noted the three steps that resulted in this global ink specialist company becoming a success story: conducting an audit to discover weaknesses in the company's efficiencies, realizing he had a skill shortage, and realizing he needed to allow his employees to give input into the daily operations of the business.[30] After correcting those deficiencies, in one year the company turned from a money loser to a highly profitable venture.

Your business, like mine, may be small but the same principles apply. Becoming brutally honest in evaluating the company's performance against your business plan and budget, surrounding yourself with people who can complement the

---

[29] Robert F. Brands is the author of *Robert's Rules of Innovation: A 10-Step Program for Corporate Survival.* I highly recommend you pick up a copy.

[30] Geller, Maurice, *Tipped for Success*, The Costco Connection, March/April 2004, p. 17

services or products you're offering, and making teambuilding a priority are not only essential for the moment but will lead to new and fresh ideas.

REALITY CHECK

At each stage of your career journey, spend time thinking of ways in which you can move your business or employee contribution a step ahead of the competition because, be assured, your competition is about to arrive. It may be tomorrow, next month or next year, but it will come. Failing to prepare is preparing to fail. That's old advice but perhaps truer than ever. Here are some tips to stay one step ahead of the game:

- It's essential to always keep on top of your job and/or business; the competition and the market will!
- A knife dulls quickly without consistent sharpening.
- Knowledge and technology are growing by leaps and bounds and it's essential to be alert to what is happening around us in terms of current and future employment.
- My favourite piece of advice: now that you've surrounded yourself with people who know more than you do, work with them to develop new and innovative ways of improving your products or service.

Here are some suggestions for encouraging creative thinking:

- Remember the definition of innovation: it includes the ability to think outside the box, to go beyond the conventional, and to try out different solutions.
- Determine to make innovation central to all your company/business planning and growth.
- Write down your idea of the dream project, marketing

approach, or out-of-the-box product. Describe how that would look.

- For everyone's benefit, and if you haven't already done it, have each employee or trusted peer sign a Mutual Non-Disclosure document before discussing, developing, or launching into any new project. I routinely have every person who works with me sign an MND prior to beginning any contract.
- Maintain a free flow of information between those employees and/or trusted peers.
- Necessity is still the mother of invention, and innovation is absolutely vital for success.
- Be an innovative team leader. If you hire other people, determine to be the best team leader possible, and that includes encouraging your people to contribute their ideas.
- Listen to the ideas they contribute!

THINGS I'VE LEARNED

- Innovation is hard work but it is exciting.
- Never stop looking for new ways to do established things better.
- Innovation is creative. I know a married couple who each run a totally separate business; one is a carpenter, the other a chef and caterer. They have one business card with one side each dedicated to the two companies. Each side has its own logo and design and each service is clearly defined.

SOMETHING TO THINK ABOUT

What sets your company apart from the competition? Does anything do that?

Have you ever pondered or, better still, discussed with a

trusted mentor or employee how to bump up your product or service to new levels of quality, uniqueness, or customer satisfaction?

Are you currently and actively discussing or pursuing an innovative new product or approach to the services you offer the market?

If so, go for it! If not, why not?

3
SECTION
DEFENDING YOUR PRIORITIES

12 Things to Discard

Wasted Time

> *"Your life is valuable so don't waste it living someone else's life."*
>
> —*Steve Jobs*

If you're like me, hours of valuable time can slip away through various Time Wasters such as those listed below. There probably is no greater challenge to overcome than eliminating the causes of wasted time.

Here are a few of the more common things to avoid:

Time Waster #1: Lack of Planning	**Suggested Solutions**
Day-to-day crises take over. This is an all too common challenge in operating a home-based business.	Keep a log of time spent on activities for at least one working week. Identify the chief causes of wasted time.
Deadlines are not set.	Unmet deadlines are a sure-fire way of losing the trust of clients and the reputation of your business.

Goals, if set, are not well defined.	Implement a policy of achieving SMART goals: Specific Measurable Attainable Realistic Timely Set daily, weekly and monthly plans.
Perception that time spent on planning is wasted.	Evaluate your progress on a weekly basis in order to see how you might improve. Also do a monthly and quarterly review of success in reaching goals. Do your priority work at the times of your peak energy.
Continual checking of email, Facebook, LinkedIn, news sites, etc.	As difficult as it may be, try to schedule the time(s) you check these sources of information, as appropriate. Some work demands continual surveillance of email, for example.

Time Waster #2: Procrastination	**Suggested Solutions**
Lack of planning and setting of priorities, objectives and strategies	Pick one area where procrastination plagues you and focus on conquering that one. Set a deadline for yourself.
Prefer doing pleasant or easier tasks	Tackle the most difficult or unpleasant task first thing each day or when your energy level is at its highest.
Thinking you don't have time to complete a task	Always do your best, but don't let perfectionism be the excuse for not finishing the task.
Allowing unnecessary interruptions to interfere with getting the job done	Do one task at a time and finish it. This brings a sense of accomplishment as well as the ability to cross it off your to-do list.
Feeling guilty about spending time on yourself	It's important to look after yourself and your health. It's just as important that you plan time to do that rather than simply neglecting another task.

Lack of confidence or fear of failure	Create an Encouragement File and review it when you're feeling less than adequate. Remind yourself of the skills and talents you itemized when you first began this journey. If those things don't help, call your mentor or a supportive friend to remind you of your strengths or offer counsel on getting through the "block."

Time Waster #3: Tyranny of the Urgent	**Suggested Solutions**
Daily tasks tend to push planned goals into the background.	Determine your priorities, objectives, and strategies ahead of time and tackle them in order at the beginning of your work day.
We sometimes think creating "urgent" tasks will satisfy our need for accomplishment (i.e. unnecessary multi-tasking) and create a false sense of "working better under pressure."	Working under pressure may get the job done, but often the work is not our best or even, inferior. Learn to adhere to a well-thought-out order of priorities; nothing but a genuine emergency is more important.

We think we have learned to function best by "crisis management."	Insist on a quiet time each day. Use this time to read, pray, meditate, go for a walk—anything that doesn't interrupt your daily retreat.
We allow all the things we think we "should" do to avoid planning the things we must do to succeed.	Decide what you are **not** going to do. Decide what work can be delegated. For example, hiring someone to clean the house or do yard work not only provides work for someone else, it relieves you of stress. Oh yes, another thing, it's impossible to sit on every volunteer board that is looking for help.
"When you are up to your ears in alligators, it's hard to remember that your objective is to drain the swamp."	Decide whether your choices have been based on what is most important … or just the most interesting. Set goals accordingly.
We have been conditioned to be task-oriented rather than process-oriented.	This is where focus and careful planning are vital. One suggestion: use planning software to help you put tasks into their proper place in the process.

We focus on accomplishing rather than becoming.	This is another powerful reason for setting time aside each day just to "be."

Time Waster #4: Socializing	**Suggested Solutions**
Friends or neighbours who have more time to visit than you do	Set your own time limit for socializing. This includes limiting time spent on tea, lunches, and meetings that cut into work time too often.
An "open door" policy	Determine when you will be available for socializing and stick to it.
Inability to say no	Initiate visits—it's easier to leave than to request that visitors do so.
Lack of an assigned value for your own time	Close the "open door" and recognize that your time has both personal and monetary value.
Lack of a daily plan	Keep an up-to-date calendar (electronic or otherwise) of all appointments. This will avoid conflicts or forgotten commitments.

Avoidance of dealing with important tasks	Become sensitive to your own needs—physical, social, work-related, emotional, and spiritual. Assign value to them and plan time for their realization.
Lack of self-discipline	Plan. Set goals. Reward yourself when you reach a goal. Be accountable to someone who will hold you to your word and commitment.
Putting the needs of others ahead of your own	Again, a regular quiet time to call to mind your value to family, friends, to God and to yourself. Unless you care for yourself, you will not be able to adequately care for anyone else. Think about the emergency procedure talk on every flight—put on your own oxygen mask before attempting to minister to others.

Time Waster #5: Telephone and Internet	**Suggested Solutions**
They are both accessible and/or part of your work.	Telephone, Internet, and social media are necessary tools in today's world. Learn to use them effectively by scheduling your response to emails or telephone calls. Limit the number of times per day that you visit Facebook.
Reluctance or the seeming inability to terminate calls	Imagine you're working for someone else and you're accountable to them for time spent on the telephone, especially on personal calls. Use the same technique to limit calls for your business as you would for theirs.
Unable to separate social and business calls and/or messages and texts	Make your friends aware that you are not available for social calls during specified hours. Set up an email account that is used strictly for either business or personal communication, but not both.

Fear of offending	Prepare a written response that is gracious, professional but also firm. Suggestion: join Toastmasters—you will receive valuable experience in making all kinds of speeches.
Lack of self-discipline	Self-discipline, like the muscles of the body, must be developed. Basically, it is learning to live by a creed of thoughtful decisions rather than being motivated by feelings and/or cravings.
A desire to escape from dealing with other tasks	Create a priority list for daily tasks but break it up with rewards between tasks. For example, after I check off a few items on my list, I give myself the choice of going on a short walk or of enjoying a pre-arranged appointment with a friend. When making the appointment, set out the amount of time you have to visit and stick to it.
Social interaction, especially from a home-based business.	Set boundaries; I know of no other solution.

Other Things to Discard

Toxic Relationships

As difficult and even gut-wrenching as it can be, get rid of toxic relationships. They only pull you down and poison your attitudes and progress. These may come in the form of people who are or are becoming jealous of your success. On the other hand, you may be the source of a negative emotional reaction that taints any interaction with that person or persons. If it can't be worked out, remove yourself from the situation.

The "Right" to Dwell on Past Injustices

No matter how deeply you or I have been hurt, dwelling on past injustices has no value. It may fuel us to some kind of action, but usually not the right kind. It's good to remember that bitterness or anger hurt *us* far more than the perpetrator of the offense.

The Sense that You Must Respond to Every Need that Presents Itself

I love to give, and I have been blessed as I have blessed others. In all that, however, I have learned that there will always be people and/or organizations that approach you with hands out. Asking you to donate a product or service within your budget is well and good; requests to pony up whenever they have a need, are not.

Lessons I've Learned

- Being gracious and forgiving isn't the same thing as allowing myself to become a doormat
- Forgiveness has to extend to ourselves, and we're often the ones least likely to receive it.
- It's not easy to turn down requests to serve on committees and boards, especially those whose values and ideals you support. It's may be challenging but there

comes a time when it is necessary.

- Looking back to "what used to be" or staring sideways at "what might have been" hinders our ability to see ahead to "all that life can be."
- Nobody or nothing is more valuable than the peace that comes from knowing I am doing exactly what I was meant to do.

SOMETHING TO THINK ABOUT

Is there an issue, circumstance or person in your life that drags you down? Here are a few ideas to deal with them:

- If you've tried but been unable to resolve the situation on your own, turn to a trusted friend, family member, spiritual counsellor or mentor … but be willing to listen and take advice
- If you find taking the first step in a process of reconciliation too difficult to face alone, see the above suggestion and ask them to go with you.
- Honestly evaluate the situation to see what lessons there are for you to learn, but then move on. Someone once said that only fools keep repeating the same process while expecting different results.

13 Things to Guard

"It is better to live rich, than to die rich."

Boswell's *Life of Dr. Johnson*

Relationships That Matter

Family

Never get too busy for family; when push comes to shove, there are no more important persons in your world. Take time to celebrate them, share with them, to just be with them. Children grow up too quickly while parents and grandparents reach the end of their lives too soon. Treasure each one while you can.

True Friends

To me, trusted friends and tested friendships are valuable beyond words or monetary wealth. If it is in your power, don't ever let them down. Whether friends are nearby or across the globe, find ways of keeping in touch for they, next to your family, are the most important people in your world.

Mentor-Mentee

A mentor may or may not be a person with whom you share social events, but never forget that they have given of their time and energy to further your career. Listen to their advice, honour their contribution, respect their boundaries and look for tangible ways to say thank you. They deserve it.

YOUR PERSONAL INTEGRITY

Don't sell it for a few bucks; no amount of money is worth the loss of trust, dignity, or even of a valued relationship. You may end up paying a price for your refusal to compromise your personal, religious, political, or work ethics, but the alternative costs far more in the long run. Remember, you will be the one most difficult to live with if you allow yourself to be bought out.

YOUR HEALTH

A lot has already been said on this subject, so, in a nutshell: look after yourself because be assured that probably no one else will.

HOLD ON TO WHAT YOU KNOW TO BE TRUE.

Believe in the beautiful things that were deposited in you, even before birth. You are one of a kind, a special ornament, a unique individual created to be a shining example of God's creative genius. Believe in that and don't let it go.

I saved this story until the end, not because it was one of those celebrated surprises one encounters with a successful career change, but because it was, I am sure, the cruelest and most difficult thing I've had to deal with in my journey. When I confided to someone I trusted that I was going to launch my freelance writing business, the comment that followed wounded me as few things have: "Writers are a dime a dozen. You'll never make it!"

I've never forgotten that, but thankfully the sting has long been removed from my heart. At that very moment I determined

I would "make it," if for no other reason than to prove to that person that I could succeed.

THINGS I'VE LEARNED

- Don't let other people determine your attitude, at least not for any length of time.
- Some criticism is wise counsel and best accepted and acted upon; other criticism is motivated by jealousy and doesn't deserve to be dwelt upon.
- Both kinds of criticism can hurt deeply, so the secret is in determining the source and intent and responding appropriately.
- Because I know what discouragement feels like, I have made it a habit to deliberately phone, write, or email encouraging messages to others on a regular basis.

SOMETHING TO THINK ABOUT

If you have areas of your life in which you have been tempted to compromise, create a list of the benefits and risks that giving in would bring. Steadfast determination to do things right is as essential to success as financial planning. You may recoup a monetary loss, but a loss of reputation and character might be irreparable. Is it really worth it?

Epilogue

"The greatest pleasure in life is doing what people say you cannot do."

—Walter Bagehot

It's been nearly thirteen years now since I made those first tentative calls to editors and administrators, and nearly thirteen years since I woke up one morning, sick and broken. A mixture of anticipation, fear, anger, and confusion swirled in my stomach; unstoppable tears coursed down my face. I was in this situation by circumstance, not choice, but I was determined by the grace of God that I would not be beaten. The first steps meant moving beyond my emotions to a new dimension of trust.

As I was to find out, there's a huge difference between working in the world of the church and non-profit organizations and competing in the world of business. What didn't change, though, was the faithfulness of God and my dependence on Him. Though I thought I knew Him well, these experiences drove me to Him in ways I couldn't have imagined, nor would I have chosen. That was then. The reality today is that He has walked with me through every step of the journey.

I am grateful for the measure of success, and I admit I that get a real kick out of saying, "I did it!"

In closing, my greatest hope in writing this book is that you will be inspired and helped in your quest to be successful.

Author Linda Wegner would love to hear from you! She may be reached via:

Email: linda@wordsofworth.ca

Website: www.wordsofworth.ca

APPENDIX A

FINANCIAL PLANNING SAMPLE TEMPLATES

Although there is no need to repeat what I've said throughout this book, here it is anyway: one of the smartest moves I made when launching my business was to engage a respected and trusted accountant. Not only has this relieved me of bookkeeping responsibilities, it has provided a sense of comfort in knowing that the latest information on matters such as taxes, employee deductions and charitable donations has been incorporated into my statements. Even so, I watch my monthly income and expenses carefully to ensure they're kept in balance; if I can't pay for it, either in full or on an approved monthly plan, I don't buy it.

My business is small, but I have no regrets in incurring this expense; the peace of mind as well as the accuracy of my annual government income tax returns more than makes up for the cost.

The templates that follow were created by a friend and mentor to me and many other individuals with businesses in the start-up phase. They are, obviously, for a hypothetical company but the information is relevant. Whether or not you choose to engage an accountant, using these templates will give you a good tool in gauging your company's profit and loss, cash flow, and balance sheet numbers.

Definitions of terminology used with these templates was found at www.investopedia.com.

Profit and Loss Forecast

Definition: this statement categorizes revenues, costs and expenses incurred over a specified time period. These statements reflect the ability of a company to earn a profit by increasing revenues and/or reducing costs. Profit and Loss statements can be used to determine the level of sales that are required to break even. These statements are also called Income Statements, or Income and Expense Statements.

	Q 1	Q2	Q3	Q4	Total
Sales	$10,000	$20,000	$40,000	$80,000	$150,000
Cost of Sales					
Inventory - open	$0	$11,000	$22,000	$45,000	$0
Purchases	$15,000	$20,000	$40,000	$80,000	$155,000
Production costs	$1,000	$2,000	$4,000	$8,000	$15,000
Depreciation	$6,000	$6,000	$6,000	$6,000	$24,000
Sub total	$22,000	$39,000	$72,000	$139,000	$194,000
Inventory - close	$11,000	$22,000	$45,000	$90,000	$90,000
Net cost of Sales	$11,000	$17,000	$27,000	$49,000	$104,000
Gross Margin (Loss)	($1,000)	$3,000	$13,000	$31,000	$46,000
% gross margin	-10.0%	15.0%	32.5%	38.8%	30.7%
SG&A Expenses					
Marketing & Selling	$1,500	$3,500	$5,000	$8,000	$18,000
General	$500	$500	$1,000	$1,500	$3,500
Administration	$750	$750	$1,500	$2,000	$21,500
Total expenses	$2,750	$4,750	$7,500	$11,500	$26,500
Net Earnings (Loss)	($3,750)	($1,750)	$5,500	$19,500	$19,500
% net earnings	-37.5%	-8.8%	13.8%	24.4%	13.0%

Cost of Sales includes the company's opening inventory measured as the cost to produce or purchase that inventory. Closing inventory is subtracted from opening inventory and purchases to accurately reflect the level of inventory used to produce goods for the finite period.

Purchases can be goods for resale or material inputs for manufacturing.

Production costs include direct labour and all other costs directly related to the manufacture of the company's goods or services for sale.

Depreciation depicts the wear and tear on fixed assets with CRA established guidelines.

Gross Margin (loss) can also be called gross profit. Percentage gross margin can be compared with industry averages to determine whether or not the company is competitive.

Selling, General & Administrative Expenses are costs such as advertising, telephone, sales & administrative staff, legal, accounting, office supplies, postage, etc.

Percentage net earnings can be compared to industry norms to determine competitiveness.

In addition, unless the company makes a reasonable return to justify the risk, it might be a wiser decision not to proceed with an investment in this venture.

Cash Flow Forecast

Definition: a financial statement that depicts the inflow of revenue versus the outflow of expenses during a specific time period. These statements express a business's results or plans in terms of cash in or cash out without adjusting for accrued revenues and expenses. Unlike the profit and loss statement, a cash flow analysis will not tell you whether or not a company is profitable, but it does show the cash position of the company at any given point in time.

	Start Up	Q1	Q2	Q3	Q4	Total
Source of Funds						
Cashflow from Operations						
Net Earnings		($3,750)	($1,750)	$5,500	$19,500	$19,500
Add: Depreciation		$6,000	$6,000	$6,000	$6,000	$24,000
Total Cashflow		$2,250	$4,250	$11,500	$25,500	$43,500
Mortgage Loan		$250,000	$0	$0	$0	$250,000
Equity Investment	$75,000	$0	$0	$0	$0	$75,000
Total Sources of Funds	$75,000	$252,250	$4,250	$11,500	$25,500	$368,500
Use of Funds						
Plant & Equipment		$300,000	$0	$0	$0	$300,000
Payments - Mortgage loan		$6,000	$6,000	$6,000	$6,000	$24,000
Total Use of Funds	$0	$306,000	$6,000	$6,000	$6,000	$324,000
Increase (Decrease)- Working Capital	$75,000	-$53,750	-$1,750	$5,500	$19,500	$44,500
Working Capital - Open	$0	$75,000	$21,250	$19,500	$25,000	$0
Working Capital - Close	$75,000	$21,250	$19,500	$25,000	$44,500	$44,500

Net Earnings are derived from the bottom line of the Profit & Loss Statement.

Depreciation is added back to reflect that this is a non cash item that is used to derive the net earnings in the Profit & Loss statement. Loan proceeds and equity investments also add to the available cash for operations.

Use of Funds includes plant and equipment costs and loan payments. You will note that loan payments are a real cash expense as opposed to depreciation that is used in the Profit & Loss statement.

Increase (Decrease) in working capital is the difference between total source of funds and use of funds.

The balance sheet, income statement and statement of cash flows are the most important financial statements produced by a company. While each is important in its own right, they are meant to be analyzed together.

Balance Sheet

Definition: a financial statement that summarizes a company's assets, liabilities, and shareholders' equity at a specific point in time. These three segments provide investors/lenders with a snapshot of what the companyowns and owes and how much the owners have invested in the company.

The balance sheet must adhere to the following formula: **Assets = Liabilities + Shareholders' Equity**

	Opening	Q1	Q2	Q3	Q4
Current Assets					
Cash	$75,000	$9,750	($7,100)	($29,800)	($66,300)
Accounts receivable (60days)	$0	$6,700	$13,400	$26,800	$53,600
Inventory	$0	$11,000	$22,000	$45,000	$90,000
Total current assets	$75,000	$27,450	$28,300	$42,000	$77,300
Current Liabilities					
Line of credit	$0	$0	$0	$0	$0
Accounts payable (30days)	$0	$6,200	$8,800	$17,000	$32,800
Total current liabilities	$0	$6,200	$8,800	$17,000	$32,800
Working Capital	$75,000	$21,250	$19,500	$25,000	$44,500
Fixed Assets					
Plant & equipment	$0	$300,000	$300,000	$300,000	$300,000
Accumulated depreciation	$0	($6,000)	($12,000)	($18,000)	($24,000)
Net fixed assets	$0	$294,000	$288,000	$282,000	$276,000
Long Term Debt					
Mortgage loan	$0	$244,000	$238,000	$232,000	$226,000
Net Assets	$75,000	$71,250	$69,500	$75,000	$94,500
Shareholders' Equity					
Capital stock	$75,000	$75,000	$75,000	$75,000	$75,000
Retained earnings (Deficit)	$0	($3,750)	($5,500)	$0	$19,500
Total Equity	$75,000	$71,250	$69,500	$75,000	$94,500

Current Assets: denote assets that include cash, accounts receivable, and inventory. Inventory represents goods that will be sold and converted into cash. Inventory is always valued at cost.

Current Liabilities: denote liabilities which are payable in the near future, such as, accounts payable and bank loan payments.

Working Capital is simply current assets less current liabilities. It is a quick indication of a company's ability to meet its current obligations.

Fixed Assets: denote assets that are acquired for permanent use in the business, such as, plant, equipment, furniture, and land. Assets are depreciated over time according to CRA guidelines reflecting wear and tear.

Long-Term Debt: denotes the value of long-term loans less the current portion that is reflected in current liabilities.

Shareholders' Equity: denotes cash or in-kind contributions made by the owners/investors. Retained earnings are a measure of net profit or loss that the company has attained over the previous period.

Appendix B

SUCCESSION PLANNING

Succession planning is another important element of a well-run business. Since I have not developed an organized plan regarding the longevity of Words of Worth, however, I cannot offer any of my own experiences or advice on the matter. My involvement in planning for the sale or disposal of my company has been limited to mentioning that it is available to the right buyer and keeping my eyes open for someone I consider suitable. In terms of the latter, I have contacted one prospective writer and university-trained researcher. Perhaps succession planning will be the subject of my next book. In the meantime, check out the following resources:

- Your local employment counselling office or business enterprise centre
- Your personal or business financial planner
- Download a free succession planning guide at: http://www.rbcroyalbank.com/commercial/advice/business=succession